125

Opening the Lotus

Also by Sandy Boucher

Assaults & Rituals
Heartwomen
The Notebooks of Leni Clare
Turning the Wheel

Opening the Lotus

*A Woman's Guide
to Buddhism*

Sandy Boucher

Beacon Press
Boston

Beacon Press
25 Beacon Street
Boston, Massachusetts 02108-2892

Beacon Press books
are published under the auspices of
the Unitarian Universalist Association of Congregations.

Photograph of The Water and Moon Kuan-yin Bodhisattva (34–10)
is reproduced by permission of The Nelson-Atkins Museum of Art,
Kansas City, Missouri (Purchase: Nelson Trust).

02 01 00 99 98   8 7 6 5 4 3 2

Text design by Wesley B. Tanner/Passim Editions
Composition by Wilsted & Taylor

Library of Congress Cataloging-in-Publication Data
Boucher, Sandy.
    Opening the lotus : a woman's guide to Buddhism / Sandy Boucher.
        p. cm.
    Includes index.
    ISBN 0-8070-7308-3 (cloth)
    ISBN 0-8070-7309-1 (paper)
    1. Buddhist Women—Religious life. I. Title.
  BQ5450.B68   1997
  294.3'082—dc21   96-45214

For Barbara Wilt

Contents

Acknowledgments

My gratitude goes to the Buddhist teachers who have guided me in my practice and to the many women and men with whom I have shared and continue to share my spiritual path. Thanks to Ellyn Kaschak and Nan Fink for reading this manuscript in an early form and to Yvonne Rand, Pema Chodron, Maylie Scott, Thynn Thynn, Ruth Denison, and Joanna Macy for going over the finished manuscript to check for errors of fact and interpretation. The Wandering Menstruals lent their support during the writing of this book, in many gestures that I gratefully remember.

I *The Heart of the Matter: Buddhist Basics*

You have opened this book because you are curious.

You know something about Buddhism: perhaps you have some experience of Buddhist meditation or have visited a Buddhist center. Maybe you read a book or article on an aspect of Buddhist practice. You may have been drawn to a Buddhist painting or sculpture and wondered about the deities represented there. Perhaps a friend of yours has told you about her or his chanting practice. Maybe a famous teacher like Thich Nhat Hanh or the Dalai Lama came through town and you heard his message of peace and nonviolence. You may know that Buddhism stresses compassion, the interrelationship of all life, and the practice of lovingkindness, and you may wonder how Buddhists express these concepts.

If you grew up, as most of us did, outside the Buddhist tradition, you may ask how Buddhism compares to other religions, particularly in its relationship to women.

I remember my own first experience with the power of Buddhist meditation and perspective. It happened in the Mojave Desert of California in 1980, in a collection of little low buildings huddled under the sweeping desert sky. I was traveling with a dear friend, a feminist and healer, who was delighted to have found a female Buddhist teacher. This teacher, Ruth Denison, led the women and men in meditation sessions focused on awareness of our bodies. She guided us in slow movements designed to develop our concentration. I remember my restlessness in the sitting meditation, my body so unused to staying perfectly still. Once I escaped to run recklessly out through the desert, dodging creosote bushes and yelling wildly just to let off the accumulated tension. Another day, rain fell on the pale desert earth, and we wandered through a storm at night to find our way back to the little house in which we were staying.

In the evening sessions Ruth Denison talked about fear, jealousy, anger, and how to approach them in our lives. She guided us in the effort to be aware—or "mindful," as she put it—of each aspect of our present experience. When I came back from this retreat, I felt spacious and peaceful, able to meet the everyday challenges of my life more easily. And I was filled with curiosity about this phenomenon known as Buddhism.

Some people I know have done Buddhist meditation for years without the slightest curiosity about the spiritual, social, or historical context in which this meditation exists. They have separated the practice from the tradition. It's a very American maneuver, deriving perhaps from our distrust of the religions we know or from our desire for efficiency, wanting only that which seems directly applicable to our lives and discarding the rest. No doubt this modus operandi works for many people, but it did not fit my particular cast of mind.

In the early 1970s, I had awakened to an awareness that the

conditions of my life were fundamentally connected to, affected by, and in part determined by the conditions experienced by all other women. That understanding made me want to grasp the total picture, that is, to discover the contours of the largest human/social/political/historical pattern in which my own life operated. I saw myself not as an isolated individual but as part of a vast community of women with similar problems and goals, within a larger community of men, women, and children throughout the world.

Likewise, when I began to sit each morning on a pillow on the floor and follow Ruth Denison's instructions to pay attention to my physical self, I suspected that I had opened the door to a whole world of experience, wisdom, and lore. I wanted to discover its extent, its depth, its particularities. Previously I had understood the relevance of politics to my own daily life, experiencing how what is done in the chambers of government, in the courts of law, in the streets of cities impacted the choices available to me and even my own view of myself. Now, encountering Buddhism, I suspected that its tenets, its long history in Asian countries, its many configurations in the United States would determine and shed light on my experience as I attempted to clarify my mind through meditation.

In beginning to study Buddhist texts, I soon found that the canon and scholarship are so vast, the traditions so various, the historical and cultural manifestations so complex that no one, certainly not I, could grasp it all. This was thrilling to me and oddly reassuring: to know that I was entering a field so rich, deep and wide that it could never be exhausted. And powerfully, through every movement toward understanding of Buddhism, I felt the truth and piercing beauty of its view of human existence.

I'm hoping that you, my reader, will be drawn to that view and will find a comparable delight in the vitality and richness of the Buddhist ideas in this book.

My engagement with Buddhist meditation and teachings has profoundly changed my life. When I think of Buddhism, I feel joy bubbling up inside. I sense the possibility of great clarity and happiness. I remember moments of peace so expansive that they allowed me to welcome and accept everything that flowed through me.

Because of this I am moved to write this book.

Almost ten years ago, in the attempt to deal with some of the difficulties I encountered in Buddhist environments and teachings, I wrote a much longer book about the phenomenon of American women's involvement in Buddhist practice. Then I went out to talk about this subject in many public places. Women asked me questions about the aspects of Buddhism they found most curious or troubling, and I tried to answer them. Women called me from all over the country to tell me of their experiences in Buddhist settings; they were encountering instances of subtle sexism or even sexual abuse and felt isolated in their communities, in which loyalty to the teacher and/or desire to maintain the status quo tended to stifle legitimate questioning. I tried to offer them something that could help: a name to call, a journal article to read, support for the courage to speak up.

In this spirit of participation in the community of women everywhere, *Opening the Lotus* attempts to respond to the questions and to meet the concerns of women like you who are wondering about Buddhist practice, about the people who pursue it, and the teachings on which it is based. As I begin, I find myself humbled by the task, for all my practice and study have led me to a very limited understanding of the huge repository of spiritual knowledge that is Buddhism.

What I am able to offer you is determined not only by my relative ignorance but to some extent by the conditions of my own particular life. I come of Scotch/Irish/English heritage, born in 1936. I grew up in Ohio, where I attended the Methodist church; as a child, I was struck by the story of the Good Samaritan, and for years hoped I could act as compassionately in my own life. But in high school I stopped going to church and decided I was an agnostic like my father, for that seemed a more hip identity than a church-going Christian. Still, at moments I wondered if God did really exist, and if I was making a mistake. College at Ohio State University helped me become more comfortable with my nonbeliever status.

Determined to be a writer, I left Ohio to work in the publishing industry in New York City, then took off to travel in Europe where I spent many hours appreciating glorious monuments to Christianity. In France I married a touring American, and we went to live and work in Barcelona for a year. When we came back to the United States and established ourselves in the San Francisco Bay Area, I settled into a life of office work to support myself and put my husband through school, pursuing my own writing to feed my deeper needs. During the ten years of my marriage I found myself drawn to texts from Eastern spiritual contexts.

At the beginning of the 1970s, I left my husband and job to plunge into the activism of the women's liberation movement, became a Lesbian, and eschewed all contact with conventional religious or spiritual thought. The 1980s brought me an awareness of and commitment to the Buddhist path. I traveled in Asia, particularly in Southeast Asia where most people are Buddhists, and lived for a short time as a Buddhist nun.

As the 1980s ended, I earned a degree in religion from the Graduate Theological Union in Berkeley, where I came to appreciate the spiritual depth and feminist insight of many Christian and Jewish women. I earn my living as a writer and teacher of writing, and I share my erotic and domestic life with women. Although I have lived in the San Francisco Bay Area for more than thirty-five years, I still sometimes feel like the Midwesterner I was.

In Buddhism, I have pursued the practice of *Vipassana* meditation; and while I have sat Zen and studied in a Tibetan Buddhist institute, I am most knowledgeable about the tradition of Theravada Buddhism (of which Vipassana is the meditation practice). My feminist perspective also colors what I am able to understand and convey. I am convinced that women are entitled, simply by being human beings, to all that Buddhism has to offer; for instance, spiritual attainment, institutional responsibility and leadership, religious validation, and support for our practice. I also affirm all that women have to offer to Buddhism and acknowledge our essential engagement in the

Buddhist path since its inception twenty-five hundred years ago.

So I invite you to ponder with me some of the great insights of Buddhism and confront some of the difficulties its practice may present for women. May *Opening the Lotus* be a doorway for you into a new view of the world.

What Is Buddhism?

What we call Buddhism began in the India of the sixth century B.C.E. It came from the heightened awareness of a human being, Siddhartha Gautama, later to be referred to as the Buddha. As a young man the Buddha, through meditation, achieved liberation from the states of mind that cause suffering. He entered into the unconditioned, boundless mind-state that is called *Nirvana*. After this enlightenment, he lived for many years, during which he established a monastic order of men and women. He wandered the countryside and gave talks known as *sutras*. These discourses were preserved at first orally by his monks and nuns, and then—four centuries after his death—in writing.

The teachings of the Buddha took hold in India, then spread throughout Asia until, in our present day, millions of people worldwide follow the Buddha way. Most of them live in Japan, Korea, Thailand, Burma, Sri Lanka, Cambodia, Vietnam, India, even Communist China, and other Asian countries. But there are also millions of Westerners—Europeans and Americans, Australians and Canadians—who have found their way to Buddhist meditation and philosophy.

One challenge in speaking of Buddhism is that the numerous traditions that have developed in specific cultures may follow different practices and put forth slightly different teachings.

Many different forms of Buddhist observance exist in the United States. Southeast Asian and North Asian immigrants maintain their own temples and practice traditional, usually devotional, Buddhism as it developed in their home countries. Native North Americans are generally more attracted to meditation than devotion. They may practice and study with Asian teachers who have adapted their teachings to Western students, or they may learn from Westerners who have trained in Asia or Western Buddhist centers. But all traditions of Buddhism adhere to certain basic principles grounded in the teachings of the Buddha. And that foundation seems a good place to begin.

THE BUDDHA WAS A HUMAN BEING

Unlike the Christian and Jewish traditions, Buddhism does not acknowledge the existence of a creator-god or require obeisance to that god. The Buddha himself was a human being. When I began to meditate, this was very encouraging to me, for if the Buddha was a *person* and able to attain enlightenment or liberation, then it was possible that I too could, through my own efforts, experience an enlightened state of mind.

When people bow to the Buddha statue that sits on the altar in the meditation hall, they are acknowledging the potential for enlightened mind that exists in each of us.

The Buddha himself urged his followers not to simply accept his ideas but to investigate their own experience and believe only that which they themselves could verify through meditation and study. So the Buddha way is not a path of received truths but a path of investigation of the human condition through one's own experience of it.

It is even said, in a Zen Buddhist text, "If you meet the Buddha on the road, kill him." This shocking statement conveys the message that no teacher can do our work for us and that extreme reverence for a teacher or a set of beliefs may keep us from reaching our own truth.

NOT "PEOPLE OF THE BOOK"

Many prominent religious traditions rely strongly on a single text. Christians take their truths from the Bible; Jews, from the Torah. Followers of Islam believe that the teachings of the Koran are literally the word of god, not to be interpreted or analyzed but followed precisely.

Buddhism offers a different model. While there is a Buddhist canon, a set of books officially recognized as containing the basic teachings (including the sutras, which are supposed to be the historical Buddha's words), Buddhists in the various traditions may use any of the thousands of Buddhist texts in the canon as a guide. Zen Buddhists may study the Japanese author Dogen; Theravada Buddhists may read the sutras; Tibetan Buddhists may refer to the wisdom teachings of Padmasambhava, the Indian teacher who brought Buddhism to Tibet, and so on. These books are respected, studied, and consulted by Buddhist practitioners, but they are seen as guides only. The pursuit of Buddhism lives in the intention and energies of the individual. It is our own efforts, whether sitting in meditation or trying to act out the tenets of Buddhism in the world, that will lead us to a deeper view of existence.

Taking Refuge

Does Buddhist practice offer any safety or comfort, you may wonder?

A Seed Falls on Fertile Ground

One Sunday afternoon in the early 1980s, my friend Treelight persuaded me to go to a chanting session at the Nyingma Institute, a Buddhist center. I was lured there principally by the prospect of the vegetarian dinner that would follow the chanting. But as we entered the center I was caught by a sign announcing the topic of the lecture to be given after dinner: "Samsara."

Samsara was defined on the poster as "worldly existence," or the usual conditions of our lives. For no reason I can understand, those words electrified me. I felt as if every cell of my body had come alive and was jangling in alarm. Pay attention! my body shouted.

I participated in the chanting and the dinner as best I could, but most of me kept repeating "samsara" and waited eagerly to hear more. Then I had to argue with Treelight, who had assumed we would skip the lecture and go home. "No, you can go but I must stay!" I told her, somewhat amazed at my own urgency.

Finally we all settled in the meditation hall for the lecture, given by a rather scholarly looking Western man and illustrated by a painting of a wheel held by a demon on which were drawn

The Buddhist path does provide strong support for spiritual practice. Most Buddhist retreats open with the reciting of the "three refuges," affirmations of our potential on the spiritual path.

1. **"I take refuge in the Buddha."**

The Buddha represents enlightened mind. When I "take refuge" in that liberated mind, I acknowledge that it is possible for me to attain deep insight and peace. There is a sort of relaxation in this, and encouragement: Yes, I too can open to moments of balance and joy and hope to cultivate them as a permanent state.

the figures of human beings performing various actions such as giving birth, rowing a boat, meditating, lying on a sickbed.

The lecturer described samsara: he told of how everything in our world is determined by conditions, that nothing exists in and of itself but only as a result of other things coming together or falling apart. He showed how little free choice we have in our lives, for most of our choices are motivated by discomfort or suffering. In every image and explanation I saw myself, trapped in response to situations I had not created and could not control. The lecturer's words shone an excruciatingly strong light on my existence. My whole body felt pain as I looked at the treadmill of conditioned actions and so-called choices that constituted my life.

I left Nyingma Institute that night shaken. And I determined to seek out the Buddhist teachings and practices that might help me develop some control over the actions and directions of my daily life.

2. "I take refuge in the Dharma."

Dharma is a word that most of us have heard or read before. When we chant this in the meditation hall, the Dharma means the Buddhist teachings, all those words of the Buddha and the other great teachers and commentators that point the way to liberation. The Buddha described the attitudes and actions that can lead one toward clarity of mind. We are guided and supported by this body of material.

Dharma also has a more inclusive meaning: "All That Is."

So when I take refuge in the Dharma, I place myself under the protection of the teachings and of all that exists in the phenomenal world. This implies a friendly, accepting relationship with the "world out there" and the "world in here": with trees and animals, people, insects, snakes, cars, airplanes, weapons, buildings, freeways, flowers, oceans, birds, ghosts, extraterrestrials—everything in the universe—and in my internal universe also. In taking refuge in the Dharma, I agree not to fight the world, gobble it up, or reject it, but to allow everything to exist along with me.

This acceptance may set the mental conditions for the "softening" that can come with meditation, a softening to one's own being, a tenderness toward and appreciation of oneself with all one's imperfections, and ultimately an appreciation that extends out to the world around us.

3. "I take refuge in the Sangha."

The word *Sangha* is Sanskrit for community. Originally it meant the congregation of monks and nuns established by the Buddha and is still often used to refer to the monastic establishment. But in the West it has come to mean the groups of mostly laypeople who come together to meditate and practice the Buddha way.

Although there is a strong tradition of solitary meditation—we have all heard of meditators sitting alone in caves in the mountains for decades, and the Buddha himself achieved enlightenment while meditating under a tree, all by himself—the dimension of community in Buddhism is as important as the concept of enlightened mind and the teachings or the path toward it.

Sometimes in the meditation hall of Ruth Denison we say:

"I take refuge in the enlightened mind.
"I take refuge in the way leading to it.
"I take refuge in the company of those who walk
    this path with me."

Those who share my hours of sitting on the pillow, who discuss with me the teachings and their own experience, who eat in silence with me, who cook the food, clean the rooms, sweep the walk, and do all the other tasks that keep a Buddhist center going—these people share something precious with me. They are my sangha sisters and brothers.

They offer me support in many obvious and subtle ways. Sometimes just the presence of other human beings is sustaining. Now and then if I look sideways in the meditation hall I may see tears streaming down a person's face, and I am reminded of the sorrows all of us carry inside; a person may come to my aid in the food line as a bowl threatens to tip and spill its contents, and I am grateful, recognizing the generosity and mindfulness possible in all of us. Someone's questioning may spark my own insight, someone's confusion or anger may lead me to a deeper awareness of my own emotions.

A number of my sister and brother meditators I see only in retreats and know nothing of their personal lives, yet I feel a

Another Kind of Sangha Sister

When I first began to meditate, I had what I can only call a vision. I am a person who rarely glimpses the dimensions of mystical experience. But one morning, as I sat erect on my pillow, I became aware of a being on the other side of the earth. She wore a dove-gray robe; her head was closely shaved, her facial features Asian; and she was sitting in meditation just as I was. I felt the solidity and depth of her spiritual capacities, and somehow she supported my own practice and encouraged me.

For days and months I sat with the awareness of this "sangha sister" far across the globe, and the strength of her practice helped me persevere in the sometimes difficult beginning stages of my own meditation.

Years later, on a trip to Asia, I met Buddhist nuns from Hong Kong and Taiwan—the other side of the world. With their robes of a soft gray, their shaven heads, they looked exactly like my meditation companion of the early days. Perhaps I was tuning in to the vast deep psychic stream that is lived Buddhism and finding just what I needed, a companion to strengthen me in my first efforts.

closeness with them. Even if I am meditating alone in my living room, I can feel that I have thousands, millions of companions on this path.

A Way of Life

Buddhism offers a great deal more than a meditation practice for controlling stress or making oneself a happier person. Its teachings can inform every aspect of one's life, opening one to insight and peacefulness in daily living. Three dimensions exist in which to cultivate one's awareness: morality, dharma study, and meditation.

"Morality" in the United States may be seen as the territory of dour clergyfolk or beady-eyed political extremists, a strait-jacket of arbitrary standards of right and wrong. But in Buddhism the word simply refers to the guidelines for conduct that we hold in ourselves, by which we assess our behavior as we move through our days. One of the principal moral teachings of Buddhism is generosity (often called *dana*) and another is the practice of compassion toward one's sister beings. These Buddhist ideals are not arbitrary but are based upon the core understanding that every living being is connected to every other.

Imagine a great net spread through the universe. Each juncture is a "being," and if we imagine that consciousness as a drop of dew, we can see that in each shining drop resides the reflection of every other drop on the net.

So we share our existence with all that exists, including animals, birds, fish, insects, trees, rocks, stars. Christianity and Judaism see "man" as superior to all the other creatures of the earth; the Bible states that god gave him "dominion over the fish of the sea, and over the fowl of the air, and over the cattle, and over all the earth, and over every thing that creepeth upon the earth" (Genesis 1:26, *The New Oxford Annotated Bible*). Buddhists have a very different relationship to the living creatures that inhabit the earth. It is not a dominating but a being-with, in which each creature is allowed to live out its life span with the least possible interference from people. The Buddha himself was said to have been an animal in some of his previous lives; wonderful stories, called *The Jataka Tales*, recount the adventures of animal heroes like the Monkey King

The Buddha Helps the Starving Lion

One story illustrates the Buddhist relationship to animals and its understanding that all life is interconnected, interdependent, and equally precious.

The Buddha, in human form, was walking out across a drought-stricken landscape, when at the foot of a cliff he came upon a mother lion and her cubs. The bones of her haunches protruded under her mangy coat; she was weak, desperate with hunger. Her cubs, similarly emaciated, lay at her feet, exhausted and near death.

The Buddha knew that the ravages of the long-standing drought had decimated the lioness's usual prey. Because she was starving, her milk had dried up and she could not feed her babies. Filled with compassion for the suffering animals, the Bud-

and the Lord of the Deer who were the Buddha in his previous lifetimes.

The Precepts

The ethical or moral tenets of Buddhism are well defined in the
Five Precepts, which are a guide to daily living. These simply
stated rules, outlined below, are practical measures to help us
proceed on our path. They are not commandments from god,
and there is no punishment for breaking them, except the recognition of what we have done in our own hearts and minds.
The rewards for following them come not from outside but
from our own reflection.

In reality the precepts are impossible to keep, for one would
have to possess the insight and discipline of a buddha to follow
them fully. But in the effort to remember and live up to them

*dha stood watching them. He saw the lioness pacing, driven mad
by hunger. He watched her come near to one of the cubs, lean
down to it, sniff it, then turn quickly away to pace again. And he
knew that the mother lion, frantic to survive, was going to kill
and eat her own baby.*

*Understanding immediately what must be done, the Buddha
climbed to the top of the cliff, directly above the lioness. Then he
threw himself from the cliff, and when he landed the lioness
feasted on his dead body and was soon able to suckle her
children.*

we learn about the world and ourselves and may find ways to do good instead of harm.

For instance, an ant walks across the desk where I sit writing. My first instinct is to crush it. But because I have so often said to myself that I am not to take life, I watch the ant instead of killing it. Implicit in my not-killing is my understanding that this tiny insect has as much right as I to live her life. And watching her, an individual with instincts, habits, desires, and a destination here on my desk, I may experience our connection as living beings who breathe the same air, partake of the same physical elements, and form part of the great net of being.

A more sticky example arises if, for instance, I feel powerfully sexually attracted to someone at my office. Let's say the person I am attracted to is a man I know is married and the father of children. I also know that he is as drawn to me as I am to him. I am married myself, and life at home feels a little boring lately. We could easily manage to "work late" one afternoon and go to a motel for some exciting sex. I am sorely tempted, telling myself that no one would ever know.

But I hesitate, for I have accepted the precept that forbids "sexual misconduct." As I step back to look at the situation, I see the potential for suffering in it. If his wife or my husband were to discover what was going on, they would be deeply hurt. Perhaps the discovery would shake our marriages to the extent that the children too would suffer. If the people in the office suspected, gossip would begin, jealousy and perhaps anger would arise. We might even lose our jobs, putting our families' economic safety in jeopardy.

I see that my action could start a chain of cause and effect that would touch many people. I would be putting in motion actions and results that would be impossible to stop and would surely cause me as much suffering as it caused the others. I decide to control my desire.

When we begin a meditation retreat we are asked to "take the precepts," to promise to abide by these rules for the duration of the retreat. But, ideally, we will follow these guidelines every day of our lives.

1. Not to kill.

This may seem easy, until you are plagued by a mosquito in the middle of the night, or you open your garage door to see the pointed snout and bright eyes of a rat peeking from behind a shovel. Or you read about a brutal murder and see a picture of the sneering murderer.

In these instances your desire to kill may rise up. You want to eradicate the offending being, to cause it or him or her not to exist—for your own convenience, for your physical or mental comfort, for your safety. The injunction not to kill is not an easy one. When we want to break it, we must look into ourselves, assess our motives, and ponder the ways in which we share the lives of other creatures.

In the Theravada tradition this precept is taken very seriously. Monks are not allowed to till the soil because in digging and working the earth they would kill worms and other earth-beings. It is said that some monks carry seives in order to strain out the tiny beings in the water before they drink it. While monks and nuns are required to eat what is given to them, not to choose or reject anything, even meat, they are not allowed to eat the meat of an animal slaughtered just for them.

Laypeople are not held to so high a standard, but the attempt to honor all life forms and cause them no harm can elicit many questions in this modern existence where we so casually exterminate other beings in order to make our human lives more comfortable.

2. Not to steal.

This means do not take what is not given. In its grosser aspects, this too seems easy. Probably very few of us are in the habit of taking other people's cars, money, computers, or TV sets. But what about the routine cheating that is so accepted in our society: fudging on our income tax forms, which hides money and keeps it in our pockets rather than in the government coffers that ought to benefit all citizens; going along with the mistakes of cashiers and clerks, as long as the error is in our favor; and all the many ways in which we struggle to get what we want, knowing that this particular money or object or food or sexual encounter is meant for another person but taking it anyway.

Our culture trains us to grab, to get there faster, to acquire more than the next person, to take what we want even if that means someone else gets less. I notice this in myself particularly with food. I love eating and take great pleasure in all kinds of food, and sometimes I become greedy. "Immediate gratification" becomes my motto. Probably each of us has a particular area in which we find it hard to control our desires.

I remember an afternoon at a meditation retreat when I walked into the empty dining hall. There on a side table stood a plate of cookies. These were no ordinary cookies but homemade delights lumpy with nuts and chocolate chips. I stood looking at the cookies. Then I glanced around the hall. Everyone else was apparently practicing in the meditation hall across the yard. I was utterly alone. My first impulse was to reach forward, pick up a cookie, and take a bite. Why not? Who would know but me? Then I wondered how the cookies came to be here. My mouth literally watering as I contemplated them, I considered the possibilities: the cookies were intended as a dessert for dinner; someone would arrive soon to take them to a private session between the teacher and some guests; they were the cooks' private treat that they had forgotten to hide. Whatever the explanation, I knew that someone had placed the cookies on this table for a reason and that they were to be consumed in a situation that had nothing to do with me. I stepped back and reminded myself, "Do not take what is not given."

When we stop the reflex of taking, a space opens in which we can look at our desire and at the situation that arouses it. Is it appropriate for me to have this? Is this meant for me? What are the consequences if I take it? And we may find ourselves making different decisions than we might have before.

3. Not to lie.

Each of the five precepts seems simple, but each opens out into tremendous complexity upon closer examination. Many people believe that lies are what hold the social fabric together. We are all familiar with the "little white lies" that our mothers may have urged us to tell in order not to hurt someone's feelings. Perhaps to survive in our families as children we learned to withhold or bend the truth. Such teachings quickly become habits. We may think of ourselves as honest, upstanding people, but even a little investigation may reveal a network of dishonesties in words and actions that shores up our sense of self-righteousness.

The difficulty of keeping this precept can be felt if you try for just one day not to tell a single lie. Lying can be subtle. What *do we not say* because our listeners would not like it, even though it is the truth? How often do we give compliments we do not mean? Sometimes we soften or exaggerate the truth in order to elicit a particular response. I have found that whenever I tell myself I can't tell the truth to someone because it would hurt her or him, I am really making the decision to protect myself, not the other person. For if I say this, she/he may react with anger, may reject me, *may not like me.* We lie to be liked. To get our way. To avoid discomfort. To escape responsibility.

The attempt not to lie can make us aware, on a moment-to-moment basis, of the ways in which we withhold and distort the truth. This knowledge can lead to an examination of our reasons for doing so. And when we fully understand our behavior in relation to the truth, we may wish to change our actions.

4. To avoid sexual misconduct.

In a Buddhist retreat setting, this precept's definition is simple: We agree not to have sexual contact for the duration of the retreat. This is done to avoid the distraction, the powerful energies and drama of sexuality, in order to maintain a strong focus on spiritual practice.

Out in the world, the definition becomes more slippery, but most Buddhist teachers would agree that "sexual misconduct" includes any kind of sexual approach or liaison that causes confusion, discomfort, or pain to any of the people involved.

At times we practice self-delusion in our sexual relationships. In order to have the thrill of being desired, the comfort of physical closeness, the reassurance of being loved, we put aside the nagging realities. Maybe we know down deep that this liaison is or will be destructive to us, but we ignore that inner voice. We may know that our affair with someone will cause pain to someone else, but we try not to acknowledge that truth in order to pursue our own pleasure. The Buddhist precept asks us to put our sexual desire in its larger human context and not to create suffering either for ourselves or other people by our actions.

5. Not to take intoxicants.

The ideal mental state that Buddhists strive to achieve is one of clarity and precise attentiveness. Alcohol and other drugs tend to dull us, or unnaturally excite us, to draw a curtain across our true perception. So, drunk or stoned, we lose the opportunity to pay attention to reality.

I learned this lesson one Sunday, when I drank several mimosas (orange juice and champagne) at a brunch even though I knew I was to attend a Buddhist meditation session later in the day. Sitting in the meditation hall I struggled to stay awake, as if I were slogging through sticky mud to get to even a glimmer of focused attention. I came out of the session very impatient with myself, for the attempt to meditate after drinking had been a complete waste of time.

Mindfulness

The precepts can be seen as guides for behavior. They are also aids to mindfulness. Mindfulness is one of the most important elements of Buddhist practice. It holds a central place: without it one cannot effectively perform any of the other forms of practice, and with it all manner of insight and deepening becomes possible.

In meditation, we try to concentrate our mental energies in order to achieve a condition of relaxed, nonjudging atten-

---

Confession of a Longtime Meditator

Today, when I go to a retreat, I know what to expect. For the first few days, as I sit in the meditation hall, do slow walking meditation outside on the desert sand, as I eat and as I wash my bowl, as I brush my teeth before going to bed, I am the victim of a vivid replay of all the mistakes I have ever made in my life. I see my inadequacies; I relive my failures in technicolor; the most disgraceful, discouraging, shameful incidents in my life rise up to parade before me. Filled with self-loathing, I sit on my pillow and I ask myself why I have put myself in the way of this. I want to run away, eat chocolate, guzzle a beer, watch Roseanne *on TV — anything but this relentless, sadistic review of the history of my stupidities.*

Still I sit, determined, and I prop up my courage with the words of a beloved female Buddhist teacher: "Whatever comes, good or bad, don't make a move to avoid it!"

Several days into the retreat, as I enter the meditation hall

tiveness. In this condition we situate ourselves in this present moment, and we are paying attention to what is going on *now*.

We are not making plans for tomorrow or the rest of our lives; we are not going over an incident from our past. We are looking at what is going on inside our bodies and minds and emotions, simply watching the show without trying to manipulate it.

Ideally I would be mindful in every moment of my life. This would have great practical benefits as I would never lose my keys, forget an appointment, or trip over the phone cord. Bud-

and take my seat, I realize that something has changed. The nasty voices have stilled, the scenes of ignominy have disappeared. I feel empty, fresh, ready to attend to my breathing, to feel the weight of my body on the pillow, to hear the voice of the teacher inviting us to pay attention to the events of this moment.

Why I have to suffer this rite of passage at the beginning of each retreat is a mystery, but at moments I see a certain logic in it. Normally in ordinary life I am even-tempered and fairly cheerful; I do not spend much time or energy engaged with the more tortuous sides of my nature. So it makes sense, perhaps, that when I stop the activities of daily life to sit still, allowing myself to be vulnerable to whatever may happen, the hard, painful, discouraging material of my life has a chance to assert itself and be fully felt by me. Blessedly I know that every mental state will soon pass away, and so, as excruciating as it is, I am able to stay with it until it changes. Then a glimmer of joy awakens in me, and I am glad I was able to endure this trial again.

dhism is not an other-worldly path; it asks us to take care of business in the here and now. While washing the dishes or dressing the baby, if our mindfulness is strong, we may see into the profound nature of reality. At the very least we will have been fully alive and awake during that time.

Buddhists speak of the restless mind as if it were a monkey, perpetually active, chattering raucously, grabbing at every distraction, and frequently causing trouble by its aggressive manipulation of everything in its environment. The monkey jumps about, picks up objects and throws them down, screeches and gabbles ceaselessly. Just so, our minds leap about aimlessly, chattering at us, worrying this topic or that and then moving on to the next.

Given the distractions created by "monkey mind," attaining and sustaining any level of present-mindedness is not easy. In the peaceful setting of a retreat—meaning a period of several days or weeks when we leave our regular lives to devote ourselves full time to the cultivation of our minds, and where we do not talk or make contact with the other meditators but focus inward—mindfulness may come to us. But it is often hard-won, even in a protected retreat setting, for the monkey continues to natter at us, and we must put forth effort in order to quiet the mind.

Compassion

A key element in the sometimes difficult endeavor of cultivating mindfulness is compassion for oneself. If I cannot accept my own limitations, mistakes, imperfections, how can I arrive at and stay fully in this present moment? And how will I ever be able to feel compassion for other imperfect beings?

In Buddhist practice, therefore, we try to cultivate a spaciousness and softening of our attitudes towards ourselves. If I am able to really encounter my own human self without judgment or commentary, then perhaps I will be able to loosen my desperate grip on that self and experience the deeper reality that underlies all existence. Then I can perceive how profoundly I share my existence with other beings, and my compassion will flow out to the creatures around me, some of whom are struggling and need my help. I feed the stray cat who lives on our garage roof; I reassure an anxious student; I repot and water the dry wilting plant on my windowsill. This "feeling-with" and desire to help extends out to the suffering members of our society, even to the great trees and other living beings in the old growth forests of our globe, to our endangered environment, air, and water.

The quality of compassion holds a central place in Buddhism. You may encounter the term *bodhisattva*, which means a person who has chosen the path of compassion. The supreme bodhisattva is Avalokitesvara. Avalokitesvara, like all bodhisattvas, vowed that he would not attain to full enlightenment until every being on earth is enlightened. And he dedicated his efforts toward promoting the liberation of all beings. (Kwan Yin, the female form of Avalokitesvara, is described later in this book.)

Avalokitesvara is often depicted as having a thousand arms and a thousand eyes. The numerous eyes allow him to see the needs of the people; with his thousand arms he reaches out to alleviate suffering. Buddhists take the bodhisattva as our model and inspiration, and we recognize that he represents a shining ideal. (For instance, who among us would throw our-selves to the starving lion, as the Buddha did?)

But we also recognize that the compassionate impulse can be awakened in each of us ordinary mortals and that there are numerous real-life "bodhisattvas" in our world, many of them people who may never have heard of Buddhism. These are the people whose motives are clear, who are filled with gentleness, who step forward to offer a hand or a supportive word at the moment when we most need it. We say of someone who is ex-ceptionally, steadfastly kind and generous, "She's a real bodhi-sattva."

What Can I Expect in a Buddhist Meditation Hall?

VIPASSANA

You leave your shoes outside, among all the other shoes on racks or on the floor. You enter to find round pillows on the rug, a simple altar at the front on which sits a Buddha statue, perhaps also a statue of the female bodhisattva Kwan Yin, flowers and incense. Most of the meditators are of European-American descent. Everyone wears ordinary clothes. The teacher sits at the front, facing the meditators, legs crossed, eyes closed. You find an empty pillow and sit down, or you may sit on a chair if you need to. The idea is to keep your back straight and your body relaxed, to concentrate on your breathing, sim-ply being aware of its going in and out. The sittings usually last forty minutes or so; then the teacher rings a bell and announces "Walking meditation." This is a slow walking in which you pay attention to the movements of your body. When the teacher rings the bell again you sit down. A "dharma talk" or lecture by the teacher may follow.

TIBETAN BUDDHISM

A broad stairway leads up into a brightly painted building, above which narrow flags whip in the wind. Inside, after taking off your shoes, you are invited downstairs to a basement room. The columns and woodwork are painted a deep vibrant blue, with panels of red and gold. Pillows are placed in rows on the floor. As you sit, you see that there are many gorgeous wall hangings of silk and brocaded cloth, each containing a painting of a deity, richly dressed, seated on a lotus blossom, or perhaps standing in a dancing posture, one leg up. You smell the incense, see the chant leader settle herself on the cushion at the front. Again, most of the meditators may well be of European-American descent.

The leader rings a bell, and the men and women around you begin to chant. Their voices are pitched deep, each syllable of the chant is sung on a long slow outbreath. OM AH HUM, VAJRA GURU, PADMA SIDDHI HUM. As you chant with everyone else, it may seem that you are enveloped by sound. After a half hour of this slow deep chant, the leader rings the bell, and the chanting stops. Then all sit in silence for another half hour. In this quiet time you can feel the effects of the chanting in your body, its vibration reaching into your tissues.

ZEN

Leaving your shoes on the porch, you step inside a high-ceilinged room. A raised platform runs along each side, and on the platforms are the black zen pillows, or *zafus*. The unadorned walls are painted white. At the end of the hall is an altar with a Buddha statue, candles, and flowers. Some of the people here may be wearing long black robes, and a few of them will have shaved heads. They sit very erect and have rested one hand in the other above their crossed legs. You climb up on the platform and sit on a pillow, facing the white wall. All is utterly still in the room, with only an occasional rustle or cough to remind you that you are not alone. You focus on maintaining your posture and follow your breath.

Later a person in a black robe approaches the altar, bows three times all the way to the floor, and lights a stick of incense. While another black-robed person beats time on a wooden drum, you follow the words of the chant in the book you have been given. A few of the chants may be in Japanese, but most are in English and you have no trouble understanding.

SOKA GAKKAI (NICHIREN)

Usually held in homes, Soka Gakkai sessions often attract African-Americans, Hispanics, and Asians as well as Euro-Americans. (If you are a person of color yourself, you may feel instantly more comfortable here than in the other settings.) The only ritual object is a small wooden cabinet. It is perhaps twenty inches high, black-draped, the doors open to reveal a paper scroll with some Japanese characters on it. A woman stands to welcome all newcomers. The gathered people begin a simple chant: "NAM MYO HO REN GE KYO," which they repeat over and over for a long time while facing the little cabinet.

The rest of the meeting is taken up with talking; various people tell how the practice of this chanting in their lives has allowed them to find a good job, repair their relationship with their mate, give up alcohol or drugs. Then a Japanese woman urges the newcomers to take on the chanting practice and promises that if you chant regularly, you will reap great rewards. With two other women and a man, she sings a rousing song about the benefits of chanting. Another woman says they will come to your house to help you make one of the little cabinets, called a *gohonzon*, and start you in your practice.

SOUTHEAST ASIAN TEMPLE

At this Buddhist center, people wander casually into the small meditation hall for an afternoon sitting. At the front stands an altar with a gold buddha statue. Around the buddha head is a neon halo in shades of pink and blue. Plastic flowers stand in ornate vases on either side of the statue, and plates hold offerings of fruit, candy bars, and cookies.

Most of those attending are likely to be Asian. At the front sit men draped in long orange robes, their heads shaved, their feet bare. At the back sit women and children. The orange-robed monks sit in various postures, one slumped to the side in a doze. Now and then one of them gets up and wanders out of the room.

You sit with the women in the rear, looking at the backs of

the monks before you, experiencing firsthand the hierarchy: monks are considered more worthy of respect and veneration than are nuns, laymen, or laywomen.

As you can see, settings for Buddhist meditation vary widely. There are many more variations; for example, each of the four major schools of Tibetan Buddhism has different practices and environments, and Zen settings may differ depending upon the country (Japan, Korea, China, Vietnam) from which their practice comes. The settings and practices may seem exotic and complicated, or they may be very simple and welcoming. To get along in any of these environments you need only be quiet and respectful, be attentive to what everyone else is doing, and follow suit.

Doing a Buddhist Practice

The word "practice" covers everything that Buddhists do in their efforts to achieve clear understanding and benefit other beings: Sitting in meditation, whether in a hall or at home. Chanting with a group. Walking, eating, doing household chores. Communicating with one's office-mates. Helping a blind person onto the bus. Each of these activities becomes "practice" if one is making the effort to be fully aware, in the moment, of one's motivations and actions and their appropriateness to the situation. Last week I spoke with a Buddhist friend who had just had a baby. "How is it caring for a little girl?" I asked. She replied without hesitation, "It's twenty-four hours a day of practice." She was being called upon to pay attention to, and to act with compassionate caring toward, this tiny human being constantly throughout day and night. And she was attempting to do it, not by rote but with full presence of mind and spirit. This is Buddhist practice.

Eating can be a practice. At Dhamma Dena Desert Vipassana Center where I go for retreats, mealtimes are practice times. Silence is observed so that one can stay contained in one's self and focused on one's own experience. We gather our food and then sit contemplating it. This can be a difficult time for me, as I smell the tantalizing odors, look at the food, worry about its getting cold. Then my teacher Ruth Denison speaks, reminding us of the many conditions and labors that brought us this food, beginning with the sun's rays and the rain, the richness of the soil, the fertility of the seeds. She speaks of the farmers' efforts, the pickers, the many people who packed and transported, displayed and sold this food, and finally the cooks who prepared it. In this way she shows how a plate of vegetables and beans and cheese carries in it the energies of many people, as well as the elements that allowed for the growth of the food. So a sense of reverence may arise in me as I contemplate my food, and my hunger now is no longer in the forefront.

Ruth may then ask us to feel our hunger and our desire for the food. And she reminds us that we eat in order to sustain our bodies and have the strength to practice. Then she asks us to pick up a utensil and begin to eat.

But again, we are encouraged to eat mindfully, to put down the spoon or fork after we've filled our mouths, to be aware of our chewing and swallowing and not to pick up our forks again until our mouths are empty of food and ready to receive the next bite.

At times I have found this way of dining very frustrating, for I am used to eating quickly. But if I am able to control my greedinesss and let myself arrive in the quite delicious moment of chewing each bite, I find myself in a very peaceful state.

When all have finished eating, Ruth asks us to feel our satiety, how our bellies are full and do not require any more, and to note how different that feels from our former condition of hunger. Then the meal is finished.

In general, Buddhist practice takes an ordinary activity and brings one's full attention to it. In that way something sacred, or, one might say, fully real, is experienced. How many meals have we eaten unconsciously, not tasting the food, our minds wandering aimlessly, or our mouths chattering as we chew or forget to chew? To eat consciously or mindfully brings us in contact with ourselves and the world. "Real" simply means fully experienced: that I know what I'm doing as I do it.

The Buddha instructed his monks:

"When you breathe in, know that you breathe in,
"When you breathe out, know that you breathe
    out."

I would add, when you eat, know that you eat. When you wash up, know that you're washing. When you dress to go to work, be aware of each action. Know what you are doing. This is being fully alive in the present moment, which is all we have.

This is Buddhist practice or, we might say, Buddhist living.

All of the rituals that Buddhists do, the chants and repeated actions, the sitting quietly, the slow movement, are techniques to help us develop the capacity to be fully present in each moment of our lives. They can lead, ideally, to a reverence for all the tasks and difficulties, the suffering, the opportunities for joy of daily life.

A Practice to Begin With

*For you who have never meditated or perhaps have only just begun
to try, here is a basic form of meditation. The spirit of this meditation
derives from my time spent with a Buddhist nun who had grown up in
Germany and lived in the United States and Australia. In its form it
no doubt expresses her own personality and compassion for her students. Before "taking robes," she had lived as a wife and mother and
as manager of an extensive farm, so that her teaching is deepened by
a great deal of life experience. The form and spirit of the meditation
also comes from my long association with my own teacher, also a
woman of German extraction with much worldly experience and a
special knack for working with people new to meditation and to
Buddhism.*

But first, a word about time and place.

*Your meditation will be more rewarding if you have chosen a par-
ticular place in your house in which to sit: a room or corner where you
won't be interrupted by people, animals, phones. It should not be a
cluttered place that will remind you of all your responsibilites and
projects.*

*The time you choose should be a time when your space is quiet
and when you can be alert and responsive. Many people like the early
morning hours because they feel rested from sleep, and the noisier
activities of the household have not yet begun. Those who are not
morning people may want to meditate before going to sleep at night,*

when the activities of the day have fallen away, or upon coming home from work in the afternoon. See which time is best for you.

One trick I have learned, which I am sure would be frowned upon by many strict meditators, is to keep a small notebook and pen near my sitting cushion. At times in meditation I receive the idea for a story, the solution to a problem I've been worrying about, the exact wording of a leaflet I have to write. If I sit with this I find myself elaborating and working with the idea, trying to engrave it in my mind so that I don't forget it, completely distracted from the desired focus of my meditation. So instead I pick up the notebook and make a note. Then, relieved that the idea will be there when I want it, I am able to let go of thinking and return with fresh energy to following my breath.

MEDITATION

Seat yourself on a pillow on the floor or on a straight chair, so that your back will be straight. If you are sitting on the floor, cross your legs before you in a way that is comfortable. If your legs are stiff and your knees stick up, put pillows under them to support them. If you are on a chair, place both feet on the floor. Your hands should be relaxed, cupped in your lap.

Take a moment to feel this posture and adjust it so you can sit still for a while. You might want to begin with five or ten minutes at a time.

Close your eyes. With your internal eye, take a look at yourself, particularly noting your good qualities. See the ways in which you are strong, generous, loving, understanding. Let yourself bask in the awareness of your own value and essential goodness.

Now let these thoughts go. Return to your body, feeling its

weight upon the cushion or chair. Make a little inventory of
your physical self: Are you comfortable? Do you feel tension?
Are you restless already? Don't try to change or suppress your
discomfort; simply allow it to exist. Soften to it and just let it be
there in you.

Now draw your attention from your body and focus it on
your breath. The movement of the breath continues throughout every moment of our lives. This inbreathing and out-
breathing is essential for our survival. If we stopped breathing
even for a few minutes we would die or irrevocably injure ourselves. Breathing also connects us with the element of air,
which enters our body and penetrates to nourish every cell. In
breathing, we share with most other beings in the world, who
depend upon air to sustain their lives. Thus our very breathing
may remind us of the interconnectedness of all that exists.

You might first wish to focus your attention upon your
belly, which lifts with each inbreath and goes flat again with
the outbreath. Notice this lifting and falling of your abdomen.
Don't adjust your breath to make it deeper or shallower. Instead just watch the natural movement of your belly, up and
down, up and down. Stay with this focus as long as you can.

Your mind will wander. It will pull you away into thinking,
planning, remembering. When this happens, notice that you
are thinking. You might even want to silently say to yourself,
"Thinking." Then gently bring your consciousness back to the
movement of your belly as the breath goes in and out.

A second place to watch the breath is at the nostrils where
it enters and leaves the body. Here the movement is more subtle

than in the belly. See whether you can feel the touch of your breath on your upper lip, just where it enters your nose. Focus on the nostrils and observe the sensations there as your nose receives the air, draws it in, and then lets it flow out again. Do not alter your breathing pattern but simply be aware of it.

Realize that you do not need to do anything, only to observe the doing. Imagine watching a baby sleep. You don't want to wake the baby, but you are fascinated with it, so you maintain a relaxed stillness, and you simply watch the lifting and falling of the baby's chest as it sleeps and breathes. In this manner observe your own breath entering and leaving your nostrils.

As with the focus on your belly, you will be able to sustain this awareness for only a short time and then "monkey mind" will leap in to amuse you or torment you or send you spinning in obsessive circles. Notice that this is happening; you may want to say to yourself "Thinking" or "Planning," and then bring your attention back to your nostrils.

This movement back and forth will tell you a great deal about how your mind works, and in the moments when you are able to be still and simply watch your breath you may experience a peacefulness.

BEFORE MAKING ANY JUDGMENTS ON YOUR MEDITATION—READ THIS!

Please remember that there is no perfect way to meditate. However distracted or restless you may have found yourself, you did not fail. Even if you experienced the attention to the breath and the attendant calmness for just one second out of five or ten minutes, you still kept your promise to yourself to meditate for that period. You stayed present to yourself and paid attention as best you could. In that effort you moved closer to who you are and honored yourself.

A Korean Buddhist master has said that the goal of practice is to become intimate with oneself. Meditation brings us to a close, at times painful, at other times joyful or neutral, intimacy with ourselves. In this there is no judgment.

When you sit down to meditate the next time, you may have quite a different experience than you did the first time. You may find yourself more concentrated and less distracted, or you may be caught up in a maelstrom of thoughts and feelings. Whatever the experience is, do your best to attend to it and return to the breath. Take comfort in the fact that meditation offers many surprises and that the more you can stay with yourself and work on your concentration, the more you will be rewarded.

Try to make time for a period of meditation each day. It will help you center and calm yourself.

II | *The Dance of Gender*

Buddhism has traditionally been a male-dominated religion. That characteristic extends both to most temples or centers in Asia and to those founded by Asian immigrants, which tend to be headed by male teachers. Buddhist centers that cater mostly to Westerners are more open to women's leadership. In Zen centers you will see women officiating as priests and giving dharma talks. In Vipassana settings, many women have distinguished themselves as teachers. Tibetan Buddhism relies heavily upon the leadership of male lamas from Tibet. Now and then a female lama is recognized, but this is rare. Very often in Buddhist settings—as in other religious traditions and also secular institutions—women may be given responsibilities and earn leadership positions while the power to make decisions and guide the institution remains in the hands of men.

It may take you a while, in any particular Buddhist environment, to understand the dynamics of leadership. A seemingly egalitarian situation may turn out to be tightly controlled by men, with women participating only as underlings and enablers. On the other hand, an institution that may seem hierarchical and excluding of female input may in practice offer women greater opportunities.

I personally believe that an egalitarian Buddhist institution is possible only if the very top leader or teacher is a woman, and one with socially enlightened views. This is not to dismiss or diminish the status and contribution of women in centers headed by men. They have struggled diligently and valiantly to break down male hierarchies and open the way for women, often with considerable success. But the symbolic significance of looking up to see, at the front of the room, yet again, a man, simply reinforces ingrained social patterns. The assumptions that gather around a male leader like a gang of sprites, reach deep into the conditioning of his female followers and elicit a subservience that may be obvious or subtle but is extremely hard to shake.

Already in our young American Buddhism, we have seen a tradition of strong women teachers. There have been several "generations" of female teachers, and it is possible to find and study with most of these women now.

Women Teachers

THE FIRST GENERATION

Teachers like Maurine Stuart Roshi of the Cambridge Buddhist Association, Roshi Jiyu Kennett of Shasta Abbey, Ruth Denison of Dhamma Dena Desert Vipassana Center, Ayya Khema of the Nuns Island, Prabhasa Dharma Roshi of the International Zen Institute, and Charlotte Joko Beck of the San Diego Zen Center have been part of the Buddhist scene in the

United States for twenty years or more. They were part of the
generation of teachers who studied with Asian masters and
founded centers in which students could practice. Some of this
generation of women, now in their sixties or seventies (Stuart
died some years ago), kept to traditional practices; some were
quite innovative in their incorporation of Western elements
into meditation practice. At least part of what they represent
and were able to accomplish came from their experience as
women, their flexibility, their nurturing and compassionate relationship with their students.

THE SECOND GENERATION

The women who came next, also seasoned with decades of
practice and teaching, offer Buddhist practice in newly relaxed
and adaptive forms. They include Toni Packer of the
Springwater Center; Yvonne Rand of Goat-in-the-Road; Sylvia
Boorstein of Spirit Rock; Barbara Rhodes of the Providence
Zen Center; Thynn Thynn, Sarah Grayson, Christina Feldman;
Pema Chodron of Gampo Abbey; Tsultrim Allione of Tara
Mandala; Arinna Weisman, Julie Wester, Sarah Harding, and
others. Many of these women are concerned with making the
practice more accessible to ordinary Americans; some seek to
combine spiritual practice with social service.

It was important to me when I first began practicing to have a
woman teacher, for several reasons. First, as a feminist activist,
I was used to working with women and trusting women. It felt
natural to seek the guidance of a spiritually seasoned woman.
Then also, having had experience with male authority figures

all my life, I did not want to have to deal with yet another, no matter how wisely or gently he told me what to do.

Some women have been sexually molested as children or sexually abused as adult women by men, or have experienced battery at the hands of men. These women often do not feel safe in male-dominated environments. When they become interested in meditation practice, they look for a female teacher.

Another reason that many women seek out a woman teacher is the conviction that women are differently connected to life than are men. In this view, women have a heightened sensitivity to nature, to human beings and other beings, and a different way of experiencing truth or reality; thus they may offer the Buddhist teachings in ways more compatible with women students' needs.

If you are interested in contacting and working with a woman teacher, refer to the Resources section at the end of this book for names and suggestions on how to find a teacher near you.

Who Is Welcome?

One of the most beautiful aspects of my early encounters with Buddhism was that, whatever environment I entered, I was welcomed and given a place. It was clear that Buddhism is for everyone, for me as well as for the people there who knew more about it. Perhaps I was particularly moved by this warmth of welcome because in my early life I had often felt like an outsider. To be received and given a place in a group came to me like a gift and a teaching in itself.

I felt this as I watched my first teacher, Ruth Denison, in

her dealings with students. I have been a careful person where human relationships are concerned. I don't leap easily into intimacy, particularly with people in authority; so I stood back and watched Ruth Denison for a long time to see if she was a trustworthy teacher. One of the first qualities I observed in her was that she treated everyone the same. Whether she was interacting with a movie producer from Los Angeles, a mentally disturbed man, an African-American Lesbian in boots and Levi's, or a young mother, she responded with steady warmth and attentiveness, and I could discern no difference in her attitude based on anyone's appearance, profession, or income. She seemed to see past each person's physical characteristics and worldly baggage to the deeper, more authentic person inside.

But while I felt, and continue to feel, welcome in Buddhist settings, I saw that there were people who did *not* feel welcomed or comfortable in Buddhist environments. People of color sometimes encounter unacknowledged, unconscious, and subtle racism. Some meditators of working-class backgrounds like myself have encountered assumptions that alienated us, like the expectation that everyone has ample funds and leisure time to devote to practice. As a Lesbian, I have always been comfortable in Ruth Denison's sangha, but I have sometimes received the confidences of Lesbian and gay meditators objecting to the subtle heterosexist assumptions of other Buddhist teachers or the homophobia expressed in some Buddhist settings.

In recent years Buddhist sanghas oriented to Westerners have been challenged to develop their consciousness of difference and to open themselves more to the input of people other than mainstream white middle-class Americans. (The immigrant sanghas are people of color, of course, and a white American might feel out of place among them. And Soka Gakkai, which has quite a diverse following, is unusual in its outreach to and appeal to the poor and people of color.) An organization called the Interracial Buddhist Council was formed on the West Coast to address issues of inclusivity and to probe race differences in Buddhist contexts. Including both white people and people of color in its membership, it offers discussion meetings and retreats. (For address, see Resources.)

A few women teachers such as Arinna Weisman in Massachusetts offer retreats just for Lesbians, and there are ongoing Lesbian meditation groups in some communities, such as the one led by Carol Newhouse in the San Francisco Bay Area. Class differences have rarely been confronted by Buddhist groups and teachers, but a few voices now and then speak up on this issue.

In no way do the Buddhist teachings serve to exclude anyone from receiving the instruction. Like Jesus, the Buddha welcomed everyone, even those people considered unclean or beneath notice by the prevailing Hindu religion: women, prostitutes, sick people, criminals, beggars, and members of the untouchable caste. Some of his enlightened teachers came from these groups.

Most Buddhist teachers I have known have been extremely open to all people and accepting of all lifestyles. A few teachers and some of the people who sit in Buddhist centers may hold prejudiced views that, even if not openly expressed, may subtly invade and infect. As the Buddha taught us, all people are victims of greed, hatred, and delusion and often act in wrong, uninformed, aggressive, and uncaring ways.

On the other hand, because we are human beings, we also have the capacity for lovingkindness and compassion to other beings, the welling up of sympathetic joy for the good fortune of others, the quality of equanimity or peaceful evenhandedness in ourselves. I find most Buddhists to be people who are sincerely trying to be good, who struggle to know the reality of any situation in which they find themselves, who go out of their way to be compassionate to other people.

If you feel welcome and accepted among the members of a particular sangha, then perhaps these are the people who will be your companions on your spiritual path. If, for whatever reason you feel uncomfortable, you may wish to talk to the teacher or practice leader about your perceptions, or you may seek out another Buddhist group for meditation that will suit you better.

Do Women Do It Differently?

Do women take a distinctive approach to the elements of the Buddhist path? I believe they do, because our life experience differs in many respects from men's.

Girls receive early social conditioning that is, in most cases, different from the training of little boys; women encounter particular expectations, dangers, and obstacles as well as encouragement to develop specific qualities in themselves, perform certain roles, follow particular paths. Because of this conditioning, the inner life of women is bound to be different from the subjective universe of most men. Certainly women are ca-

pable of doing any work that men do, and we have the examples
of female doctors, lawyers, electricians, athletes, carpenters,
CEOs, spiritual teachers, ministers, scholars, and scientists to
convince us that no intellectual, spiritual, or physical achievement lies outside the realm of women's abilities. But we can
surmise that women in these professions may approach their
work in a distinctive manner or may view its practice and significance differently from their male colleagues. In some cases
women's participation may change the nature of the profession itself.

Greeting the Sun

*When I was first practicing with Ruth Denison, we participated
in a ritual each morning at her retreat center. We would walk
before dawn to the* zendo, *or meditation hall, a small concrete
block structure bitterly cold in the darkness. Bundling ourselves
in shawls, we sat on our pillows in silent meditation. Ruth Denison sat before us in her long dress, a cap over her hair.*

*Just when the windows began to lighten, Ruth would ring
the bell and lead us outside. We walked out, our feet crunching
on the desert sand, and arranged ourselves in a circle among the
spindly creosote bushes dipping in the wind. Then we turned to
face the east, which had begun to be touched with subtle colors.
The clearest blue, the mellowest gold, the palest rose hues ran
tentative fingers across the sky.*

*For a time Ruth led us in a "seeing meditation" to develop
understanding of the mechanism of seeing that we take for
granted every day. We turned slowly to gaze in every direction,*

Female spiritual teachers in the Buddhist tradition have and continue to offer the teachings in innovative and often recognizably female-oriented ways.

Women may take a more psychological approach to teaching, adapting their message to the twentieth-century, psychologically-oriented conciousnesses of their students.

Women teachers may be more accepting of the expression of emotion by their students. Some women practitioners tell of spending time in male-run environments where emotions were suppressed, and then going to a female teacher who encouraged them to acknowledge and fully experience whatever strong feelings might be coming up in them.

registering the "form and color" of the vast desert, the distant mountains, and the closer focus of bushes and rocks. Then she led us in a slow dance of welcome to the sun as it bulged at the horizon and finally burst up, flooding the sky with glorious light. Soon our bodies had become warm from the movement and the rays of the rising sun.

Ruth spoke of the cycles of the moon and sun, the alternation of night and day. She invited us to greet this new day as an opportunity to develop our mindfulness, deepen our awareness and appreciation of our own lives, and renew our commitment to the practice that could lead us to liberation. Listening to her voice, I felt at once strongly concentrated and hugely expanded, as if my mind and body held the whole desert and sky, the fresh breeze, the distant small sounds of other humans waking and beginning their day. I felt passionately, completely alive and grateful.

Often women teachers do not limit themselves to the traditional forms of practice but strike out to devise new methods
or incorporate elements of other traditions. At a woman-led
retreat you may find yourself dancing in a circle, reaching to
the sky, touching the ground. You may be led on journeys of
guided imagery. You may be invited to pay particular attention
to the natural environment in which you practice, noting the
life of trees, animals, rocks and streams and how this is interre-
lated with your own life.

How Have Feminists Affected American Buddhism?

Those of you who are interested in the issues raised by the most
recent women's movement may wonder whether it has made a
mark on the institutions and practices of American Buddhism.
The answer is a definite yes.

Since the early 1980s, two groups of women have come together in Buddhist practice situations, though sometimes with
difficulty: the women who had dedicated themselves early on
to Buddhist practice and institutions, and the women new to
Buddhism who had engaged in feminist political activism.
Each group brought something crucial to the mix. Feminist
women new to Buddhism insisted on equality, critique of hierarchy, identification of misogynist texts and practices, and al-
tering of sexist language. Women with years of Buddhist practice brought patience, seasoned spiritual perspective, and a
spacious view to the dialogue.

A series of conferences on Women and Buddhism, held
across the country, allowed women to break out of their
isolation and talk with other women and a few supportive

men about the issues that concerned them. They allowed us to experience the teachings of some female Buddhist "masters" who came to give talks, and we were able to discuss volatile subjects like sexual abuse by male teachers. Women expressed their differences in perspective: creative, innovative practice versus more traditional forms; insistence on equality and nonhierarchical relationships in Buddhist centers versus a trust in the usefulness of traditional hierarchical structures; incorporation of goddess worship, shamanic and Native American elements into the practice versus a holding to the pure Buddhist forms. The conferences built understanding and trust among women Buddhist practitioners of all persuasions and gave many women the sense that they were not alone but had become part of a collective questioning of the forms within American Buddhism. They drew strength to challenge oppressive or abusive situations when they identified them within their own Buddhist environments.

As a result of the persistent, courageous efforts of these women and others, many Buddhist institutions have become more sensitive to women's particular needs, more open to women's spiritual leadership, and less hierarchical in their structures.

One particularly dramatic contribution of feminism to Buddhism has been the shift in perspective on sexual power abuse by teachers. Through the efforts of determined women and a few men, the veil of secrecy previously obscuring the issue of sexual abuse has been drawn aside, and a lively public debate has ensued about how to approach such incidents.

While abuses still occur, there is much more openness in confronting and dealing with them. Some Buddhist teachers are making efforts to establish a code of conduct to which all Buddhist centers would agree to subscribe.

Can Women Be Buddhist Leaders?

If you grew up in a Catholic household, you know well that women's participation in the hierarchy of the Catholic Church is strictly circumscribed. Again and again I have heard the discouraging story of the little girl, fired by religious zeal, who asks to be the child who assists the priest at the altar. She is told that only boys can help to celebrate the mass. When those little girls grow up, they are acutely aware that only men can be priests who give the gift of God to the community.

In many Protestant denominations, through the efforts of dedicated women activists, women ministers are ordained and routinely officiate and preach in churches. In others, the doors are still closed to full participation. In some churches women are ordained but not given the full responsibilities of ministers. Lesbian women in particular find it difficult to be accepted and empowered by Protestant denominations.

Since the late 1970s, a number of women have become rabbis in the Jewish faith, generally in the more liberal synagogues and seminaries. In Orthodox settings no women are allowed to officiate. The Conservative, Reformed, and particularly the Reconstructionist or Jewish Renewal movements do allow women to become rabbis. While female rabbis still face prejudice, more and more of them are becoming the leaders of congregations. And some Lesbian rabbis also perform rabbinical duties in synagogues.

Can Buddhist women wear the robes and carry out the duties of religious celebrants? The answer is as varied as Buddhism itself.

In most Western Buddhist settings, women perform the same religious offices as men. At a Zen monastery you will see probably an equal number of women and men wearing black robes, ringing the bells, beating the drums, and giving the dharma talks.

In Vipassana settings, there is little official hierarchy; no one even wears robes (except an occasional visiting Theravada monk or nun). Women are very visible and influential in the Vipassana establishment.

Tibetan Buddhism's attitude toward women leaders is more complex. The tradition was brought to this country by maroon-robed monks in exile from their native Tibet, and in their Western sanghas, these foreign monks remain at the top of the hierarchy. But these monks have ordained Westerners, including a very few female lamas. Each of the four separate traditions or "schools" within Tibetan Buddhism takes a somewhat different approach to hierarchy and practice. Notable Tibetan Buddhist women leaders include Pema Chodron, an American woman who heads a Tibetan Buddhist monastery in Nova Scotia, and Tsultrim Allione, who has broken away from male-led groups to establish her own center and teaching schedule. Many other Tibetan Buddhist women hold positions of authority in the male-run centers, but always subordinate to male leaders.

Soka Gakkai is as open to women's leadership as men's. They operate from a Japanese model, in which women's and men's activities are often pursued separately.

The immigrant sanghas generally reflect the traditional gender hierarchy maintained in Asian cultures. Men are usually at the top, and women support their work. There are, of course, exceptions, as the sanghas become more Americanized. For example, a Japanese-American woman serves as a fully ordained priest in Shin Buddhism, a largely Japanese denomination.

Are There Goddesses in Buddhism?

Many contemporary women are intrigued by the idea of an ancient goddess culture, a time in prehistory in which women

If you have looked at Buddhist art, you've noticed that many representations of the Buddha or other embodiments have decidedly feminine characteristics: breasts, delicate facial features, softly draped clothing. Buddhists believe that as beings achieve more refined levels of enlightenment, the distinctions of sex and gender fall away, leaving a transgendered or genderless figure. Nevertheless, the Buddhas or other figures with breasts and sweet girlish smiles are always referrred to as "he." Similarly, male Buddhist teachers who have studied with or venerated female teachers or forebears may express feminine qualities in their teachings, but they retain their conventionally masculine assumptions and sense of entitlement.

shared equally with men in all dimensions of public and private life. Archeological research in the Middle East has unearthed evidence of a peaceful agricultural society in which female divinities or perhaps one divinity, the Great Goddess associated with earth and the cyclical creation of all life, were venerated. According to this theory, this egalitarian, nurturing society was conquered and taken over about five thousand years ago by peoples from a more Northern, warlike society, and the centuries of patriarchal aggression and hierarchy began. The conquerers overthrew the goddesses and enthroned a single creator-god.

However, in some religions, vestiges of the early goddess figures have survived. In Christianity, the Virgin Mary can be seen as a goddess. The Virgin of Guadalupe in Mexico City and other great virgins hold tremendous power in their particular cultures. Female saints like Joan of Arc and Teresa of Avila, while they were actual historical figures, have accumulated almost the glamour and influence of goddesses.

In Judaism the deity is sometimes called Shekinah, a feminine name. This word is used for the comforting, more personal aspect of God. The Hebrew goddess Asherah and the Canaanite goddess Astarte were worshipped in Hebrew temples before the masculine god took over. Perhaps the Shekinah is their legacy, a concession to the need to connect with and venerate female essence.

In Buddhism a number of powerful female emanations hold sway. The two best known of these, whose images you may come across, are Kwan Yin and Tara.

Kwan Yin (also spelled Quan Yin, Guan shih yin, Kannon, and Kwannon-sama), the Buddhist female embodiment of compassion, is the most revered goddess in Asia. She originated in China and is venerated in Japan, Korea, and throughout Southeast Asia. In Burma, for instance, statues of the goddess of compassion can be found in almost every home. While she is a Buddhist embodiment of the highest spiritual attainment, Kwan Yin also has the wide popularity of a folk goddess.

A lovely, playful goddess, Kwan Yin grants the wishes of those who call upon her, especially women, and exerts particular power over childbirth. Her name means "She Who Harkens to the Cries of the World," for she is the one who arrives to save people from burning buildings, pluck them from train wrecks, and to offer general relief from suffering. It is Kwan Yin who listens to the voices of the poor and oppressed.

Kwan Yin came to China from India in the form of the Buddhist Avalokitesvara, the embodiment of compassion in a male form. But as she became more Chinese, she also became more womanly, until finally she took on a completely female character and appearance. Soon she was identified with various real-life women who were discovered to be deities after their deaths. When Kwan Yin assumed human and Chinese identities, she achieved a widespread national following. Some scholars believe that Kwan Yin's female nature resulted from the fusion of the qualities of Avalokitesvara with the Taoist Queen Mother of the West. Others see her origin in the early Indian, later Tibetan, goddess Tara.

First Meeting with Kwan Yin

*During a 1982 book tour, I was staying in Kansas City at the
home of a woman who invited me to go with her downtown to
the Nelson-Atkins Art Museum. "There's someone I want you
to meet," she said.*

*In the museum we entered a high-ceilinged room empty
except for a splendid wooden statue of a woman. She was
about life size, with Asian features, dressed in gorgeous
loose red trousers, a gold robe, wearing a jeweled crown,
many bracelets, and long dangling earrings. She sat with
one leg up, knee bent, foot on the seat on which she sat,
her arm balanced casually on this upraised knee. She
braced herself with her other arm. Her eyelids were nearly
closed, as if we had come upon her in some sort of relaxed
reverie.*

"How beautiful!" I burst out.

"Yes," my companion said. "This is Kwan Yin."

*"Kwan Yin," I repeated. I had never heard those words
before, had known nothing of this female figure, even though
I had begun Buddhist meditation the previous year.*

*"But who is she?" I asked, wanting historical and cultural
background, dates, scholarly references.*

*My companion chuckled. "Just be here with her, and you'll
find out."*

I gazed at the statue, somewhat annoyed.

*"You should have seen this room ten years ago," my compan-
ion offered. "It was full of hippies sitting on the floor, and you*

*could smell the weed. They'd sit here all day, just soaking in
Kwan Yin's vibes."*

*I smiled, and turned to see her eyebrows lifted in amusement.
Then she was gone, wandering off without explanation, her broad
back disappearing out the doorway. How odd to find myself so
disoriented in the Midwest, where I had grown up and thought
I knew the parameters of consciousness.*

*Well, apparently not. Here I lingered, alone with this being
whose name was—what had she said?—Kwan Yin. There was
nothing to do but look at her. I walked over to stand squarely
in front of her.*

*She sat before a wall painted in faded swirls of green and
red and yellow and white, with the dim figures of flowers, flowing cloth, clouds discernible in the colors. Her seat looked like
a rock, uneven, darkly modeled. The luxurious gold and red of
her clothing flowed down over this rock to where her bare foot
rested on a pillow that looked like a blossom. Her body was
perfectly upright, her head high even while she appeared
completely relaxed. Her face with its lowered eyelids, its
slightly smiling lips, had been carved of wood in the eleventh
or twelfth century and painted, her robe gilded. Her posture
of upraised leg, outstretched arm balanced on knee, made a
powerfully stable pattern against the swirling of the wall
painting.*

*Her serenity and power gradually reached out to me, engaged
my senses until it held me there before her, filled with something*

*like happiness and sorrow all mixed together. Mysteriously the
space between us had become palpable; indeed the whole cavern-
ous room seemed vibrant with her presence.*

*Eventually I gave up examining with my eyes the gold buckle
that held together her robe, the earrings that I now realized were
long pendulous earlobes, the lines like successive smiles on the
skin of her throat, and just took in her whole figure. The feelings
in me settled, and a stillness opened in and around me.*

*Now I understood why the flower children had come to
spend whole days in her presence. I imagined her smiling just
this way, so tenderly, as the smoke of their joints wafted up
around her. Indeed it must have reminded her of the incense
burned for her in her native temple in China, the obeisance
offered up to her by centuries of worshippers. She had come
from that distant past on the other side of the world to sit,
as tranquil as a lake on a windless day, here in a museum
on the Great Plains of America. I was grateful for her presence.*

*As I drove east the next day, leaving the expanse of the
Great Plains behind and entering the more densely populated,
industrial part of the Midwest, I kept a postcard of Kwan Yin,
bought at the museum, on the car seat next to me. Sometimes I
glanced at her, and without understanding why or how, I knew
that I had set out upon a relationship with a being who embodied
something profound, at once deeply female and universally
human.*

If you come upon statues or paintings of Kwan Yin, you will see her in one of several forms. These different embodiments of Kwan Yin derive from the Chinese appearances. The development of Kwan Yin began with Ta pei Kuan Yin (who started out in life as the Princess Miao-shan), the thousand-armed, thousand-eyed goddess of compassion (a counterpart to Avalokitesvara, who also has a thousand arms and eyes). Ta pei is later depicted with just two arms and two eyes, holding a green willow branch and a bottle of pure water or life-giving nectar, symbols of healing.

Next came Nan hai Kuan Yin, the "Kwan Yin of the South Sea," who is shown with a male and female companion and a white parrot. Sailors from the Southern port cities of China venerate her and call upon her to save them from stormy seas.

Accounts from the twelfth to the fourteenth centuries describe another manifestation, Yu-la Kuan-yin, otherwise known as "Kwan Yin with the Fish Basket," " Mr. Ma's wife," and "Kwan-Yin with Chained Bones," names deriving from the vivid stories of her arrival in people's lives. When her human embodiment died, her bones were found to be attached to each other by golden chains, a sure sign of divinity.

A surprising and provocative form of Kwan Yin was known as the "Woman of Yen-chu," a woman who gave away sex to any man who asked her, in order to free him of his unhealthy desire. She was the sensual Bodhisattva who used bodily desire to achieve enlightenment. (Learning about her, I pondered a possible connection between the Woman of Yen-chu and the temple priestesses of antiquity, whose religious duties included sexual intercourse.) Later, when the rather puritanical Confucianism became popular in China, this Kwan Yin fell into disrepute and was no longer worshipped.

Finally, there is the "White-robed Kwan Yin" (Pai-i Kuanyin), a goddess capable of granting children. Often depicted holding a baby, she was not a mother herself but represented universal motherliness. The veneration of Kwan Yin grew to include the chanting of mantras to petition White-robed Kwan Yin to grant the male children necessary for ancestor worship and funeral rites.

(This section is based on the scholarly work of Chun-fang Yu.)

THE FEMALE DIVINE IN TIBETAN BUDDHISM

In the Buddhism of Tibet, a number of female beings, divinities and others, exert a powerful influence. Buddhism in Tibet is grounded in a rich and subtly elaborated philosophy, and its practices include transformation techniques such as visualization. Some of the beings visualized are female embodiments of compassion and emptiness.

The goddess Prajnaparamita represents the crux of Buddhist philosophy. *Prajna* means wisdom; *paramita*, perfection. She is the perfection of wisdom because she signifies the essential matrix of existence—the fecund, inexhaustible "emptiness" out of which all phenomena arise. She is lauded in *The Great 25,000 Verse Prajnaparamita Sutra*, which is considered to be the originating text of the Mahayana school of Buddhism. Prajnaparamita is depicted seated in meditation, profoundly peaceful and somewhat remote in her loveliness.

There are playful female spirits as well, such as the *dakinis*.

The dakinis, who are sometimes wrathful, are usually shown in a dynamic dancing or standing position. They are "spiritual midwives" who arrive to aid the seeker by cutting through ignorance and conceptualization and offering her direct access to her own wisdom.

Other female deities are depicted as the consorts of male deities. Often they are shown embracing the larger male figure, the two joined in blissful sexual union. This posture reflects the practices of an esoteric form called Tantric Buddhism, pursued mostly among Tibetans.

TARA

The most popular and best-known Tibetan Buddhist goddess is the great Tara. Like Kwan Yin, Tara represents the quality of compassion and is seen as the female counterpart of the male celestial bodhisattva Avalokitesvara. Her name means Star, which is interpreted as "she who leads across" or the Great Saviouress. Full of compassion, she comes to the aid of people in distress and champions the downtrodden.

She is also proudly female. As the story goes, in a previous lifetime the woman who was to become Tara made a vow to help all suffering beings. Hearing of her intention, some monks told her that she could only accomplish her goal of becoming a bodhisattva if she transformed herself into a man. She refused, reminding them of the Buddhist insight that all forms, including the concepts male and female, are empty of reality (that is, they partake of the ever changing world of conditioned existence but do not reflect the deeper, unchanging reality that underlies it). Then she vowed that she would serve the aims of all worldly beings while retaining her female form. Thereafter, through many lifetimes, while perfecting her meditation, she saved countless beings from suffering. Ultimately through her efforts she became a bodhisattva, the Great Tara.

Tara shares the achievements and renown of the greatest of bodhisattvas. Practitioners meditate upon her and visualize her in order to deepen their understanding and develop their own compassionate natures. Some scholars believe that she was a model for Kwan Yin, via the Tantric Buddhist deity, White Tara. It is thought that Chinese Buddhists conflated the White Tara with Avalokitesvara and then transferred her qualities to Kwan Yin. The relationship between Tara and Kwan Yin is strongly felt in Asia.

One often sees Tara on the *thankas*, or wall hangings, in Tibetan Buddhist environments. She is depicted sitting in meditation posture on a lotus blossom. She wears an ornate headdress, earrings, necklace and bracelets, loose pants, and only a minimal draping on her upper body. Her eyes are open, looking out at the world of suffering beings. Her left hand lifts in the gesture of "all is well, do not be afraid." Her right hand opens palm-outward over her knee, indicating the granting of blessings. She holds the stem of a lotus flower in her left hand. She is often depicted in different colors—as Red Tara, White Tara, Green Tara—with each color giving a different significance. The most commonly seen Tara is the Green Tara, whose distinguishing feature is that she is ready to step forward, her right foot extended, just on the point of getting up to come to the aid of those who suffer.

Tara has existed for fourteen centuries. After the many chal-

lenges of her former lives, she is said to have been reborn as the
Great Tara from a lotus that grew in Avalokitesvara's tears of
pity. She is known as "Mother of All the Buddhas," a title that
emphasizes her wisdom, for the Buddhas are born from
wisdom.

Tara's mother-goddess nature may come from her Indian
roots for she was recognized first in that country. In India a
number of powerful mother-goddesses reign. As such she sug-
gests the great round of nature, the plants and animals, and,
more important, our capacity for spiritual transformation. She
embodies the esoteric truth that ordinary life, or samsara, and
enlightenment are one. Perhaps my powerful reaction to the
concept of samsara back at the Nyingma Institute was an in-
kling of Tara's truth.

Tara represents the culmination of the spiritual path: full
awakening or enlightenment. The lotus flower on which she
sits expresses her purity, for it grows up from the mud beneath
the water, then opens its lovely blossom in light and space
above the surface. She is associated with the moon, symbol of
the subconscious and the cyclical.

As the Goddess of Action, Green Tara rushes to the aid of
anyone in distress who calls her name. In seventh-century India she became famous for saving people from the Eight Great
Fears, manifested as lions, elephants, fire, snakes, robbers, im-
prisonment, water, and man-eating demons. The Eight Great
Fears were pride, delusion, anger, envy, wrong views, avarice,
attachment, and doubt.

Tara is a bodhisattva and buddha at the same time, fully
perfected and enlightened but staying in the world to help oth-

ers reach enlightenment. (The word *buddha* simply designates "one who has awakened," that is, who has direct understanding of the truth.) She conquers evil beings, even armies, nonviolently, without fighting.

She can manifest in many forms, the most popular being the twenty-one emanations, each designed to perform a particular function. A well-known set of verses in honor of Tara is called the *Praise in Twenty-one Homages*. Depictions of these twenty-one emanations show Tara at times as fierce and even demon-like as well as peaceful and motherly. She wields implements with multiple arms; her images are of different colors; sometimes she stands in victorious postures; sometimes she is shown with animals such as a goose or a bull.

But most commonly Tara is depicted sitting in meditation posture, her right hand open in a blessing, a lotus held in her left hand.

In both Kwan Yin and Tara one may see parallels with the Christian Virgin Mary. Both, in their compassion, resemble the gentle Virgin. In their power and autonomy each is a towering, dynamic embodiment in her own right, with wide followings among faithful Buddhists in a number of Asian countries.

The rites surrounding Tara include a chant: "OM TARA TUTTARE TURE SVAHA," which means

> Homage to Tara, the swift heroic one,
> Who eliminates fears,
> The Saviouress who grants all benefits
> Buddha to be worshipped and praised.

A Practice to Begin With

Many people who are just beginning meditation practice find walking meditation to be the most effective and centering form. The Buddha specified that one could practice meditation in four positions: sitting, walking, standing, and lying down. Walking meditation has the advantage of requiring the participation of your whole body and therefore provides ample material on which to focus your attention. It also can provide a break from sitting meditation, a respite in which you can maintain your concentration.

MEDITATION

This can be done inside or outside. The idea is to limit the scope of the walking in order to contain the mind. So just mark out for yourself a route about fifteen or twenty feet long, noting a rock or bush or couch corner that will serve as a landmark to remind you to turn around.

Stand upright with your feet together and your hands clasped loosely behind or before you. Lower your eyes so that you see the ground maybe five feet ahead. Set your intention: Walking.

Now lift one foot, move it forward, and set it down. As your foot touches the earth and your weight shifts forward, the heel of your other foot will be lifting off the ground. Let it lift, move this foot slowly forward, come down again. Be as aware as you can of these motions.

You will notice that there are three gross or large motions— lifting, moving, and setting—within which many more subtle motions are occurring. You can aid your concentration by naming or noting each movement as it occurs, so you are saying mentally, "Lifting . . . moving . . . setting," as you very slowly step forward.

Try this out. Don't worry if you wobble a bit. Don't worry if you get distracted for a moment, suddenly remembering that phone call you didn't make, or planning dinner, or noticing a bird hopping down the driveway. Just return to your concentration on this movement of walking and remind yourself what you are doing by repeating the formula: Lifting . . . moving . . . setting.

When you get to the end of the track you have set for yourself, stop, turn around, and stand for a moment, feet together, to rededicate yourself to this movement. Sometimes I say to myself, "Intention" to let myself know I am setting my intention on walking, as before.

Lift your foot and start again. You may notice all the tiny movements of your foot as it flexes and lifts, your leg carrying it, your body balancing upright, falling forward with gravity as you move your foot forward and set it on the floor. You are involved in a very complex set of actions that involves your whole body. Keep your focus on the movement of your foot while being aware of your body's involvement.

There is no need to judge yourself: "I am not doing this well," or "I'm great at this!" Try to stay with the sensations, the actual experience of walking, which precedes or lies beneath all the chatter of your mind.

If you feel the desire to look up at your surroundings, then you can do one of two things: You can let the desire pass without acting on it and keep your eyes down. Or you can make a conscious decision to look up and survey the room or countryside around you. Just be aware that you are doing this, for as long as you desire, then lower your gaze and return to your focus on your feet.

There is a fourth movement one can notice. After your foot touches the floor, you press down and the weight of your body shifts onto that foot. Almost immediately your other foot begins to lift. It was useful to me to note that shift of weight before I took the next step. But I seem to be a slow learner: I had been doing walking meditation for three years without being aware of that shift of weight. Often Ruth Denison would lead us in the walking meditation, and she would always call our attention to it, but for some reason the awareness of it did not reach me. That is, I was doing it without knowing it.

I tell this because I want you to understand that all of us move at our own pace, and the petals of our awareness sometimes open slowly, one by one, like the petals of the lotus flower. We can only know what we can know right now. The practice will open our knowing: A good teacher points the way, but even so it may take years to "get" a simple truth or experience, and we need to be lovingly patient with ourselves. I remember the moment, in the meditation hall in the desert, when suddenly I knew that I was experiencing that shift of weight. I really felt for the first time that settling of my body's heaviness down on the forward foot, and a whole new dimension of walking meditation opened for me. I also found that I exhaled naturally with that movement.

Now when I walk I note Lifting, moving, setting, shifting.

Perhaps you have noticed that I don't say *I* lift, *I* move, *I* set. That is because in my awareness of the movement of my feet— if I am really able to pay attention—I leave behind the I with whom I usually identify so strongly; that composite of traits, desires, aversions, emotions, fantasies, ego that I call my self. If I am able to be fully there in the walking, then all that exists is

Lifting, moving, setting, shifting.

Try it for ten minutes or twenty minutes at a time, and see whether it brings you to peace, or even a kind of delight.

The walking meditation I have described is the traditional Theravada form as I learned it from my teacher and from the Burmese monk U Silananda. One can approach it in many other ways. Once I visited a Western nun friend at the Burmese monastery, Taungpulu Kaba Aye, near Boulder Creek, California. On the deck under towering trees sat an emaciated, ancient man wearing the brown robe, his bony right shoulder bare, his eyes hidden behind dark glasses. This was the Venerable Taungpulu Sayadaw—a monk considered in his native Burma to be an enlightened being, an arhat or saint. Taungpulu was instructing his monks in a soft, dry voice. I asked my friend to translate, and she told me he was asking each one about his walking meditation: "Were you aware of the flex of your foot before lifting? Were you aware of the moment your heel left the ground? How often did you notice this?" and so forth. She said that each morning she too was interrogated, asked whether she had been able to identify the most

subtle mini-sensations inherent in the act of walking. And in this man-
ner Taungpulu trained his monks and my nun-friend to be meticu-
lously aware of each moment of their lives.

In contrast to this utterly traditional approach, the Vietnamese
monk and antiwar activist Thich Nhat Hanh has written a small
book called A Guide to Walking Meditation *in which he encourages*
us to combine attention to walking with attention to the breath, count-
ing steps with breaths. He introduces other techniques such as imagin-
ing a lotus flower blossoming with each of our steps. And he leads us
to feel the profound awakening and peace in simple movements of
walking meditation as well as to connect at the same time with the
suffering in our world.

But though different teachers put forth different approaches to
walking meditation, the technique described above can be a basic,
reliable method for bypassing your worries and preoccupations to
enter that most serene place in yourself, to remind yourself that it
exists always, true and sustaining.

III | *Ancient Beginnings*

The India of twenty-five hundred years ago, in which the Buddha achieved enlightenment, offered a limited number of roles for women, who were viewed as just slightly "higher" intellectually and spiritually than animals. The preeminent role was that of wife. Women were given in marriage, often as little girls, and were expected to produce sons for their husbands. (Sons were extremely important, because the funeral rites for a man had to be performed by his male heir.) Besides producing boys, the wife was expected to devote herself exclusively to the husband's service. Lower-class women also served as workers and domestic slaves. A small number of women worked as musicians and dancers, and others became courtesans.

In this very restrictive society, the Buddha offered an additional role. Women could "go forth into the homeless life," that is, they could escape the domestic sphere to become nuns and pursue a wholly religious existence. Or they could become lay devotees and patrons of the Buddha and achieve merit in this and the life to come. In these ways, women participated in Buddhist practice and institutions from the very beginning and made their mark on Buddhism's initial shape and character.

While the Buddha established a monks' order at the inception of his years of teaching, the nuns' order came into being about five years later. During those first five years laywomen had begun to follow the Buddha, to practice his teachings and to give food, clothing, and shelter to the monks. Because they were practicing diligently, it was to be expected that at some point some of them would want to leave their domestic lives and fully enter religious life.

Women renunciants were not unknown in Indian society; Mahavira of the Jain sect had already ordained thirty-six thousand women to become nuns.

How the Nuns' Order Was Founded

The Buddha's custom was to walk about the countryside accompanied by his monks and to give teachings, usually in outdoor settings like groves or parks. On one such occasion, he was approached by his own aunt and foster mother, Mahapajapati, with a group of women of his own clan, the Sakya clan. Mahapajapati told the Buddha that she and her companions wished to live the ascetic life of nuns; and they asked him to establish an order of nuns like that of the monks. The Buddha refused her, even though she asked three times. Mahapajapati, sad and discouraged, left with the women.

The Buddha went on to another town. Mahapajapati and her followers, temporarily stymied but still determined to become nuns, cut off their hair, thus signaling their renunciation of worldly life. They put on the orange robes worn by the monks and set out on the long journey to the town where the Buddha was giving a discourse. I think of this as the very first

Women's Liberation march in history. These were noble-women unused to effort or labor; the long walk was hard on them, leaving them dirty, with swollen feet, travel-worn and exhausted.

The monk Ananda saw them coming. He was shocked at their appearance, and when he heard the reason for their arrival he was impressed with their perseverance and agreed to press their case with the Buddha. Three times Ananda suggested to the Buddha that women should be allowed into the order. The Buddha remained silent. Ananda tried another tack. He appealed to the Buddha's sense of justice by asking him whether women were as able as men to achieve the highest levels of enlightenment. The Buddha replied that women were capable of attaining full enlightenment. Given this assertion, he had to agree that a monastic order should be established for women.

The Buddha told Mahapajapati that he would found an order of nuns, on the condition that she take on Eight Special Rules, which ensured the nuns' deference to the monks. She agreed, and she and her followers became the first Buddhist nuns.

Much speculation exists about the reasons for the Buddha's initial refusal to ordain nuns. He had already challenged the strictures of the society in which he lived by accepting people of low caste into his ranks, so it made sense that he would allow women to take on a religious role. Whether out of deeply ingrained cultural prejudice or other influences, the Buddha hesitated where women were concerned. But more important, he eventually *did* open the monastic life to women, and the nuns' sangha that he founded flourished for nearly a thousand years and still exists in some Asian countries.

Some of the women alive during the Buddha's lifetime achieved liberation or enlightenment; their names and accomplishments were recorded. A number of them became powerful teachers, leading large groups of female renunciants as their compassionate acts and eloquence attracted more women to the order.

Laywomen also played important roles in early Buddhism. The laypeople took a great interest in the Buddha's teachings and in the order of monks and nuns he founded. In the India of that time, the ascetic ideal was almost universally admired, so that the laypeople were receptive to the goals of the order. They took responsibility for the material support of the monks and nuns, and some wealthy laywomen became major donors to the order.

Who Were the Women of Early Buddhism?

When the women who shaved their heads and took robes had reached a sufficiently enlightened state, they began to give discourses on the teachings of the Buddha and the path to enlightenment. They gave public lectures out in the open, but they also went into the women's quarters of the houses they visited and spoke to the wives and servants there about the tenets and practices of the Buddha way. In this manner they influenced a large segment of the population and acquired many followers.

Some of them became famous teachers. Sukkha was particularly persuasive. As I. B. Horner quotes from a contemporary chronicler in *Women Under Primitive Buddhism*, Sukkha "taught the doctrine in such wise that she seemed to be giving them [a great company seated around her] sweet mead to drink, and sprinkling them with ambrosia. And they all listened to her, rapt, motionless, and intent."

A woman called Patacara, who came to the order through great personal suffering, led a large gathering of converts. The Buddha's aunt, Mahapajapati, through whose persistence the order was founded, also converted many people.

First among the great women "preachers" was Dhammadinna, her name meaning "giver of the Dharma." The Buddha, hearing of an explanation she had given on the tenets, commented, "Learning and great wisdom dwell in Dhammadinna." He added that he would have spoken just as she had, saying, "Her answer was correct and you should treasure it up accordingly."

Buddhism is among the few religions of the world that have acknowledged the identities and accomplishments of women in their official canons. I have no doubt that women were central in the establishment of all of the world religions, but their efforts and accomplishments are often hidden and their identities either expunged from the records or reduced to subordinate roles. Buddhism in its original manifestation not only benefited from the input of women but officially noted their presence and contributions.

SONGS OF THE SISTERS

In the sixth century B.C.E., when a person had an experience of enlightenment, she or he would compose a song. These lyrics were passed down in the oral tradition, as were the dis-

A Visit to the Bodhi Tree in India

We step inside the enclosure to see an enormous ancient tree, its heavy limbs propped with sticks. A four-foot-high saffron cloth wraps the base of the tree. Prayer flags flutter between its branches.

Pilgrims in their white clothes sit among shaven-headed monks in orange robes, nuns draped in white or orange cloth. Most of the seated pilgrims are women, their eyes closed in meditation. They hold a stillness. Indeed, here among all these people, all this color, there exists a deep silence. It's what I recognize in Buddhism. A gentle, open feeling, an allowing of all of us here.

I find a place among the meditating women, sit and look up at the gnarled heavy branches of the tree. The ancestor of this tree shaded Buddha as he sat day after day inviting bodhih, perfect knowledge. It witnessed his moment of enlightenment, an event now deeply embedded in time, twenty-five hundred years ago. I close my eyes and feel the profound peace of this place holding me.

After a while I begin to have something of that feeling of enclosure and stillness that I experienced on the Nuns Island in Sri Lanka. It was there that one day I slipped through a fold in time to find myself in the forests of ancient India, seeing a slim young man in an orange robe whom I knew to be the Buddha talking with his monks and the enlightened women who surrounded him. That same energy holds me, here, a feeling of a presence, some echo of the particular human beings who awoke to the light of perfect understanding so long ago.

courses and sayings of the Buddha, probably by recitation by convocations of monks and nuns. Sometime in the first century B.C.E., the songs were committed to writing and became part of the official Buddhist canon. These verses, brought together in a volume called the *Therigatha*, have been translated by a number of scholars into English. I will quote from Mrs. Rhys Davids's translation, *Psalms of the Sisters*, in this chapter.

The women represented in these seventy-three songs of liberation were of several types, and their liberation came to them in ways appropriate to their situations.

Fleeing from Domesticity. First among them were the women struggling to escape their domestic lives, who desired to follow a religious path but were prevented by parents or husbands. Usually these women stayed in the home, accepting their servitude and pursuing their spiritual practice by themselves. Often it was while preparing food, fetching water, or performing other domestic chores that the woman pierced through to illumination. Then, characteristically, her parents or husband would recognize the change in her and agree to let her join the nuns' order.

The woman would become the pupil of a *Theri* (female elder). She would live very simply and serve her teacher as a novice. Through daily lessons and prescribed meditation and exercises, she would attain liberation and thus be qualified to become a teacher and leader herself. In her enlightened state she was aware of all her past lives and thus was able to understand the inevitable gross or subtle workings of *Karma*—cause and effect—in her own present life and in the lives of others.

One woman who achieved her first deep insight in the

kitchen is referred to as "Little Sturdy" in the *Therigatha*. She
had heard the Buddha speak and wanted to join the nuns' order, but her husband would not allow her. So she stayed home
and performed all her duties while reflecting on the words of
the Buddha and cultivating insight. Then one day while she
was cooking curry, a flame shot up out of the cook fire and
burned the food to ashes. Watching the food go up in smoke,
she saw the utter impermanence of all things, and her mind
opened to enlightenment. It was only a matter of time, then,
until her husband gave in and she went to study with the great
woman teacher Pajapati. Pajapati ordained her and took her to
see the Buddha, who, knowing how she had come to realiza-
tion, sang this verse to her:

> Sleep softly, Little Sturdy, take thy rest
> At ease, wrapt in the robe thyself hast made.
> Stilled are the passions that would rage within,
> Withered as pot herbs in the oven dried.

Another woman achieved awareness of the great law of impermanence when she spilled the water she was carrying and
watched it run into the earth. Another tripped and fell, and realized that all things change.

These women, when they escaped their domestic situations, entered the homeless life and developed insight, and they
sang of the *freedom* they experienced. Their verses (or gathas)
name the goal of spiritual practice as emancipation, liberty.
Partly this is the freedom from their previous restricted lives,
partly it is freedom from the universal elements of human life

that enslave us all. Mutta, who had been given in marriage to a hunchbacked nobleman, left him, entered the order, and achieved full liberation. She sang exultantly:

> O free indeed! O gloriously free
> am I in freedom from three crooked things:
> From quern [mill for grinding grain], from mortar
>   [grinding bowl], from my crookback'd lord!
> Ay, but I'm free from rebirth and from death,
> And all that dragged me back is hurled away.

Those Who Suffered. Another group of women who came to the nuns' order were those who had experienced great disaster and loss in their lives. Chief among them, and one who became a teacher and nurturer for other grieving women, was Patacara. While she and her husband, with their small child and newborn baby, were walking through the forest to visit her family in a distant village, a storm came up. Patacara's husband went to cut shrub to build a shelter for them, while Patacara laid the children on the ground and protected them from the rain with her own body. All night long she waited for her husband, who did not return. In the morning she found his lifeless body, bitten by a snake. She wept and lamented, but finally she had to go on.

Patacara came to a river much swollen by the rain. Realizing that she could not carry both children across at once, she left the older child on the bank and crossed with the baby. Then she spread her headcloth on the ground, laid the baby on it, and started back across the stream. She kept looking back anxiously at the baby and then at the little child standing on the other bank waiting for her. Suddenly from midstream, she saw a huge hawk circling in the sky. As she watched in horror, screaming to scare it away, it swooped down, picked up the baby in its claws, and flew away with it. The older child, confused, tried to go to his mother, fell in the river, was swept downstream, and drowned.

The devastated Patacara finally came to the village where her family lived. It was her last refuge. But when she asked a villager how they were, he told her that in last night's storm the roof had fallen on them and had killed them all. At that very moment her father, mother, and brother were burning on the same funeral pyre. She could see the smoke.

Patacara went mad and wandered in circles, wailing her grief. She was despised and harassed by the townspeople, but one day the Buddha, who was giving a discourse in a nearby grove, saw her pacing in a circle in the dust, and he recognized the essential clarity of her mind. Later he walked near her, saying, "Sister, recover your presence of mind." And because his own mind-power was so strong, she immediately "came to." She fell at the Buddha's feet and told him everything that had happened to her. He spoke to her, helping her to see that through countless lifetimes she had mourned for lost loved ones, and that grief is simply part of our human condition. Patacara's sorrow lifted.

Then the Buddha taught her that human relationships cannot provide refuge or safety; wise people purify their own conduct and set out on the spiritual path. Patacara's understanding deepened and she asked to be ordained. As a nun she practiced diligently, and won through to enlightenment.

It is said that Patacara became a great teacher to all who came, particularly women who had suffered the death of a child. From her own experience of this agony and her subsequent awakening, she was able to offer comfort to these women. She was said to have five hundred followers. Later, looking back, they paid tribute to Patacara, singing:

> Lo! From my heart the hidden shaft is gone.
> The shaft that nestled there she hath removed,
> And that consuming grief for my dead child
> Which poisoned all the life of me is dead.

The Beautiful Ones. Another category of women who achieved liberation through the Buddha's influence and their own efforts were beautiful women, including courtesans, enamored of their own loveliness.

Khema, a great teacher, personifies this group. As a young woman she possessed exceptional beauty, with skin like gold, and she was consort to a king. When the Buddha came to preach in the Bamboo Grove, she would not go to see him, for she knew how infatuated she was with her own beauty and she was afraid he would disapprove of her. The king tricked her into going to the grove. There she saw the Buddha, and he recognized her excessive attachment to her body. So, using his magical powers, he created a show for her. He conjured up a lovely woman, who stood fanning him with a palm leaf. Khema was impressed, seeing that the Buddha surrounded himself with women even more beautiful than herself. But as she watched, the woman began to age, her body coarsening, her limbs weakening, her hair turning gray, her teeth loosening, her skin wrinkling. Finally the woman, in extreme old age, fell to the ground and died.

Horrified, Khema realized that if this devastation could happen to a body even more beautiful than hers, it could happen to her also.

The Buddha talked to her, contrasting the life of lust and attachment with the delight of those who have released themselves from worldly bonds. Listening, Khema achieved enlightenment.

From then on, Khema taught the Dharma and became known for her great insight. The Buddha ranked her among his most gifted disciples.

HOW THE THERIS SPEAK TO US TODAY

Though their lives are so remote from our own, both in time and cultural context, the women of early Buddhism hold great significance for those of us interested in Buddhism today.

When I first read the *Therigatha*, I became very encouraged and excited. I was thrilled to discover that these ancient women achieved the highest levels of enlightenment, a fact that lets me know I can do so too. I could identify with their struggles to escape from limiting situations and reach their full potential. The verses and commentary of the *Therigatha* attest to the women's determination, backed by courageous effort; to the depth of understanding many of them reached; and to the development of their personalities as they realized their goal. Their spiritual gifts would most probably have lain dormant if they had not been allowed to enter the order of nuns and to live a life dedicated to spiritual work. So the Buddha opened a path to women that challenged and benefited them and carries over to us today.

Then I am encouraged by how the nuns learned from each other, with a more experienced *bhikkuni* (nun) mentoring a neophyte, until the new seeker achieved a high level of enlight-

Under the Bodhi Tree

I look at the faces of the Indian women meditating near me, absolutely motionless in their pure white robes. These are the literal descendants of the women who listened to the Buddha give his lectures. It is said that during the Buddha's lifetime, many people needed only to hear him speak to reach enlightenment. I have read the verses in which the Theris, who must have looked a great deal like the women around me, sing of the moment at which they "woke up."

I listen to the chanting, surrendering to the silence that underlies it. I am so grateful to be here, for I understand that no matter how different we may appear, in skin color and size and costume, all our particularities fall away before the flame of shared humanity that burns in us, our potential for enlightened mind.

I have been welcomed and given space to flower. I feel the ancient tree, so alive in its garments of prayer flags and shiny leaves, speaking to me. I want never to leave this place.

enment and could attract and instruct her own students. In this manner a women's lineage was established in ancient India. This model can inspire us to cultivate that same giving and receiving among women in present-day life.

POWERFUL LAYWOMEN

Not all female followers of the Buddha Way wore robes and shaved their heads. Some lived in the world, wearing rich clothes and jewelry, running households as wives or consorts to men. Women were as welcome as men to attend the discourses of the Buddha, and they received the teachings enthusiastically.

We can imagine the scene, outside on a hill or in a clearing in the woods, sometimes in a park or arbor created by a nobleman or woman. The Buddha in his saffron robe, his right shoulder bare, sits in the most conspicuous spot. Surrounding him are monks and nuns and the several strata of laypeople, from the king and queen with their retinue, to nobles and rich merchants, to humble workmen, slaves, and beggars. The people sit, hushed, while the Buddha's voice speaks of the great central truths of human existence and the path to liberation from suffering. Some individuals, merely hearing his words, achieve enlightenment in that moment. Others go home to ponder what he has said and perform the practices he has taught them.

Some laywomen, rich and poor, were so struck by the Buddha's words that they became lay disciples and wished to give to the sangha of monks and nuns. Dana (generosity) is a key Buddhist concept. In gratitude for the monks' and nuns' efforts to preserve and spread the Dharma, and in recognition of the austere life they pursued, the laypeople contributed food, medicine, clothing, and dwellings when appropriate. There was a selfish element to this giving, for it was thought that in performing dana, one acquired merit, a sort of bank account in which one piled up moral funds that would insure a fortunate rebirth. But there was also the intrinsic worth of the development and practice of generosity in the people who gave.

The poorest woman might give a handful of rice; the wealthiest might build a *vihara*, or dwelling place, for the monks when they ceased their walking during the rainy season. The sangha of monks and nuns was not locked away in a monastery, far from daily life; they walked freely among the laypeople, received their food at the hands of housewives, interacted with kings and beggars. They themselves were beggars, called almsmen and almswomen because they begged for alms. "Going forth into the homeless life" (that is, being ordained) meant literally that one had no home and no material security of any kind. This lifestyle could exist only if it was supported by the surrounding society, making laypeople, women included, extremely important to the development of early Buddhism.

One influential laywoman was Visakha, who was spoken of as "The great lay Sister." The Buddha had quickly acquired a large company of monks and nuns, numbering in the thousands. The feeding, clothing, and caring for this huge group fell to patrons like Visakha. She also gave the Buddha and his sangha her friendly criticism, her sustained support in upholding the teachings and the discipline.

Visakha, daughter of a rich merchant and wife to another, invited the Buddha and his company into her house to eat. Hearing the Buddha speak, her father-in-law and mother-in-law were converted. Visakha's many children and grandchildren grew up following the Buddha Way. The Buddha set forth a moderate view, asking his almspeople to follow a simple life but not to engage in extreme austerities or mortifications, so his teachings were attractive to laypeople like Visakha. She went freely into the vihara (monastery) to hear the Buddha speak, and when she saw a monk engaging in indiscreet behavior, she did not hesitate to reprimand him. When a grandchild died, she went to the Buddha for consolation in her grief.

Through her piety and her gifts Visakha developed a certain amount of authority in the running of the order, including an influence on the changing or defining of the monastic rules. She spent vast sums, building the vihara and providing robes and medicine for the sangha. She never flagged in her support and was considered a true and faithful mother to the religion. As the Buddha himself often stayed in her town, he frequently conversed with Visakha, sometimes teaching her, sometimes asking her advice on worldly matters. A long talk between the two of them has been preserved in the sacred texts.

The laywomen were extremely important in promoting the Buddha's teachings, for they communicated them during the activities of daily life and thus reached many more people than could the Buddha in his discourses. They also, along with the laymen, validated the order by their material support. Laypeople and almspeople strove together and apart, differently and similarly, to propagate Buddha's great Truths.

How Did Buddhism Develop So Many Different Styles?

Just as Buddhism found its way to this country, so in the ancient world it was carried from its birthplace in India to the other countries in Asia. This dissemination began when the Way was introduced into Sri Lanka. Then it traveled to China and Southeast Asia around the first century C.E. In the sixth century it found its way to Japan, brought by Chinese and China enthusiasts as part of the influx of Chinese culture into Japan; in the seventh century Buddhists came from Central Asia, India, and China to bring Buddhism to Tibet.

The details of this dispersion are too numerous to report here, but some broad outlines of how the religion changed as it was established in particular cultures may help us to understand contemporary Buddhist traditions in the United States.

Several demarcations in thinking occurred early on, before the first century C.E., among the different schools in early Buddhism. The schools split into three major traditions: The Hinayana (now usually known as the Theravada, or Way of the Elders), the Mahayana, and the Vajrayana. Followers of the Mahayana (or Great Vehicle) asserted that their "vehicle" was large enough for everyone to ride in it to enlightenment, while the Hinayana path provided access to only an elite few. Thus Hinayana (Small Vehicle) became a denigrating term and is not much used today.

THERAVADA (FORMERLY HINAYANA)

Theravada Buddhism is the complex of beliefs and practices based on *The Pali Canon*, the books set to writing some four hundred years after the Buddha's birth. People in the Theravada tradition follow the Buddha's original instructions and concentrate on achieving individual enlightenment.

MAHAYANA

One of the most distinguishing characteristics of the Mahayana forms of Buddhism is the concept of the *bodhisattva*. The Mahayana practitioner begins with *bodhicitta* (aspiration) or "the mind set upon enlightenment" in a vow to become a fully enlightened Buddha. She goes through a series of stages leading to that goal, but she resolves to delay her own final liberation in order to remain in the world until all beings have been saved. The Mahayana bodhisattva works ceaselessly for the benefit of other beings and transmits to them any merit she may have generated by her own practice. The bodhisattva ideal appealed directly to the mass of the people, for the bodhisattva was a heroic, merciful being always ready to comfort and help them. Because all bodhisattvas have great loving hearts whose infinite love and compassion is extended to all beings, they serve as models to the faithful in showing the way to enlightenment. There are "celestial bodhisattvas" who are mythological in origin, and there are some historical figures who achieved the condition of the bodhisattva in their lifetimes, but the spiritual attainments are accessible to all people who diligently pursue the Mahayana path.

VAJRAYANA

A third demarcation in Buddhist belief came with a group of Buddhists who followed the Mahayana path in India but felt that individual enlightenment could be accomplished in a single lifetime rather than gradually over many lifetimes. This path requires a close devotional relationship with a guru, who passes on spiritual power through personal transmission. This kind of Buddhism is called Vajrayana, the Diamond Vehicle, or Esoteric or Tantric Buddhism. The Vajrayanists outlined the practices that lead to this-life liberation in texts called *sadhanas.*

THE THREE SCHOOLS IN THE PRESENT DAY

All three of these branches of Buddhism exist in the modern world, and the practice you pursue, the center you visit, is part of one of these schools.

Theravada Buddhism is named for the only school in original Buddhism that survived. It was the Theravada elders who wrote down the canon in the first century B.C.E. in an early literary language, Pali.

Theravada Buddhism exists today in Sri Lanka and the countries of Southeast Asia such as Thailand, Burma, Cambodia, and Laos. In the United States you will usually not see the term Theravada used, but if you study with a teacher whose major practice is Vipassana (insight meditation), you can surmise that the teacher has trained in the Theravada tradition.

The Mahayana exists in Japan, Korea, Tibet, and other parts of Asia. In this country, Zen centers and Pure Land establishments are associated with the Mahayana tradition. The Mahayana canon is written in the ancient sacred language, Sanskrit.

It is most often Tibetan Buddhists who follow the Vajrayana path, but there are esoteric schools in other countries as well, such as Shingon Buddhism in Japan. Vajrayana practice is taught in this country principally by Tibetan lamas.

These categories are not in practice mutually exclusive; in many countries, their attributes are mixed. The Mahayana, for instance, keeps some of the monastic dictums of the Theravada. Some scholars and teachers consider the Vajrayana to be part of Mahayana Buddhism rather than a separate school. Many people of Asia are more tolerant of different and seemingly opposed ideas, and may follow several spiritual paths at once. On the other hand, many Asian Theravadins, the first Buddhists, seek to maintain the original forms and beliefs of the Pali canon, free from modern, more liberal notions.

As Buddhism traveled throughout Asia in the sixth to tenth centuries, it went through many transformations. More than the other great missionary religions, such as Christianity and Islam, Buddhism has always been shaped by its surrounding culture and has integrated folk or cultural elements into its beliefs and practices. This flexibility is possible in part because Buddhism is not bound to a centralized, symbolic place: there is no Rome, no Jerusalem, no Mecca in Buddhism. Because of this decentralized nature, Buddhism can be, perhaps must be, particularly respectful of and receptive to cultural influences. Traditions such as pilgrimage to local sites where spirits dwell found their way into Buddhism. Calendric associations led to celebration of special days throughout the year, corresponding to earlier folk rituals. In some locales, caste distinctions were grafted onto the Buddhist practices. Buddhism adopted life-cycle rites in some contexts; for example, in Southeast Asia, men coming of age are required to spend time living as monks.

At a Buddhist center in the United States, you may find yourself in a setting organized around a Tibetan lama, a Burmese *Bhikku* (monk), or a Japanese Zen priest, each of whom may teach traditional practices in the traditional way. You may chant in Pali, or bow in Japanese fashion, offer a white Tibetan scarf. On the other hand, the Buddhist center you enter may be Western in all its accoutrements.

Whether it is Vietnamese immigrant families coming forward to place fruit and candy bars as offerings to a large, gold-plated Buddha on a sumptuous altar, or a Western woman in jeans seated on a pillow on a living room floor giving meditation instruction to casually dressed participants, this is living Buddhism.

How Have Women Fared in Buddhist History?

The examples of the Theris and powerful laywomen of the Buddha's lifetime notwithstanding, Buddhist texts and institutions in many cultures have discriminated against women.

There are several reasons for this. First of all, as we have noted, Buddhism took root in the Indian culture of twenty-five hundred years ago, which relegated women to a distinctly inferior status. As illuminated as the early male Buddhists were, they were still somewhat limited by traditional prejudices. The same can be said for the Buddhists of China, Japan, and the other Asian countries, whose cultures kept women in subordinate positions.

The monastic root of Buddhism also played a role in limiting women. The Buddha chose to establish first a male monastic order, in which the monks were expected to avoid all sexual contact. In order to break down or deflect the monks' desire for sensual and sexual intercourse, women were portrayed as the repositories of sensuality and therefore as obstacles to spiritual practice. Verses from the early periods, quoted here from Diana Paul's *Women in Buddhism*, reflect this prejudice.

> Women can ruin
> The precepts of purity.
> They can also ignore
> Honor and virtue.
>
> Causing one to go to hell
> They prevent rebirth in heaven
> Why should the wise
> Delight in them?

Monks were encouraged to quell their desire by imagining the physical decay of the beautiful woman's body, thus replacing lust with an awareness of the impermanence of all things. They were enjoined to keep their distance from women.

Evils are compounded
and good friends depart
When one is addicted
To women . . .

If one listens
To what I have said
They can be reborn, separated
From women.

A man's spiritual attainment was thereby measured, to some extent, by his distance from and indifference to women. Some texts go further, portraying women as inherently evil, rather than simply obstacles to men's spiritual achievement.

Ornaments on women
Show off their beauty.
But within them is great evil.

Just as a fire in a deep pit
Can cause fire damage without smoking.
A woman also can be
Cruel without pity.

The dead snake and dog
are detestable,
But women are even more
Detestable than they are.

Some scholars believe that these texts were not part of the original canon but were inserted later during a period of sexist retrenchment in India, when the notoriously oppressive Laws of Manu were put into effect. This happened during the first centuries B.C.E. and C.E., long after the Buddha's death, and may have been a Hindu reaction to the power of the Buddhist path. The Laws of Manu severely restricted Hindu women. Following that misogynist move in the society at large, these scholars argue, the Buddhist monks composed verses like the ones quoted above, denigrating women. The situation during the Buddha's lifetime would have been much more accepting of women than these damaging statements convey.

But whether or not these verses existed during the Buddha's lifetime or were later insertions into the canon, in reality the monks were often in daily contact with laywomen, maintaining a relationship of mutual respect. And when the nuns' order was established the monks counted large numbers of women among their own ranks.

Could Women Become Bodhisattvas and Buddhas?

Through many centuries of Buddhism, it was thought that in order to achieve the highest spiritual attainment, one had to be reborn in a male body. Maleness was an image of perfection: the fully realized state of bodhisattvas and buddhas. So, to attain enlightenment the woman had to change her body to that of a man and give up all future female rebirths. Thus in the Mahayana sutras (discourses), women are acknowledged as spiritual assistants to the Buddha, but they reach lower stages of development than their male counterparts.

At the same time that these texts were studied, however, illustrious female followers of the Buddha became well known

and were accepted as teachers. Women teachers like Asa, Prabhuta, and Vasumitra were lauded in documents and verses,
in which it seems that their female characteristics offered no
obstacle. Of Prabhuta, it is said (quoting again from *Women in
Buddhism*): "Aside from the Buddhas and Bodhisattvas, no one
comes to see her whom she does not overwhelm with her physical and mental superiority, the lustre of her spiritual fire, her
exquisite complexion, and her beauty. And whoever might see
the lay disciple Prabhuta—be they gods or men—know her to
be the teacher."

Clearly, the texts and their influence did not prohibit out-
standing women from teaching. Looking at the early verses for
the monks or later tracts requiring a sex change, we may come
to the conclusion that Buddhism was a highly male suprema-
cist religion. But while the influence of the texts cannot be
denied, they are balanced to some extent by the evidence of
women's active, continued participation in Buddhist monastic
and lay life.

Some women directly challenged the sex change require-
ment and won. Most famous is the Goddess Tara, described in
the previous chapter. Tara insisted on remaining a female and
attained bodhisattva status as a woman. Kwan Yin is another
example of a female bodhisattva, whose fame and worship ex-
tend through a great part of Asia.

The understanding that formed the foundation of increased liberality was that neither maleness nor femaleness
constituted an inherent or ultimately real trait, and therefore
to base any discrimination upon a person's gender was to act
in ignorance of deeper truths. A debate is recorded between a

goddess and the sage Sariputra, who had the temerity to ask her, "Why don't you change your female sex?" After instructing Sariputra that there are no innate characteristics of femaleness and therefore she could not alter them, she changed him into a woman and herself into a likeness of him. She then asked the female Sariputra, "Why don't you change your female sex?" Sariputra realized that he was not, in the deepest levels of himself, either male or female, and said so. The goddess changed him back into his male form, she became female again, and they continued their debate, or rather, her instruction of him.

In line with this mutability of gender, celestial bodhisattvas such as Kwan Yin are often viewed as potentially bisexual, able to appear in male or female form according to the expectations and need of the seeker.

In later Buddhism the Tantric tradition (Vajrayana), which shared perceptions and practices with an earlier Indian esoteric sect, fully acknowledged the transformative power of a male divine principle joined with a female divine principle. Buddhist Tantrism is the only school of Buddhism in which the interaction of feminine and masculine qualities, sometimes through sexual union, is used as a means to liberation. Some scholars believe that Tantrism dates back to the practices of the Dravidians, or earliest people of India, and is based in goddess and earth religions.

Traditionally, Buddhist scholarship has assumed that the female partner in Tantric practices was a person of lesser attainments than the male: a servant girl or prostitute who was simply being used by the man to achieve higher levels of spiritual ecstasy. But a recent book by Buddhist scholar Miranda Shaw has demonstrated that the women were as spiritually adept as the men, and in some cases more so, for instances of great female Tantric teachers are amply recorded. In her book *Passionate Enlightenment: Women in Tantric Buddhism*, Shaw has shown that women were committed to their spiritual practice, attained high levels, and were acknowledged by their contemporaries as initiates, adepts, and teachers.

How Are Women Viewed in Present-Day Buddhism?

In general, women in contempory Asia have a lower social status than men, and they receive fewer opportunities for education and development. However, they also wield many kinds of power and influence that may not be visible to the eye of a Western observer. The Asian perspective and way of life are so different from our contemporary American worldview that making general statements about Asian women's participation in Buddhism would be inappropriate.

But in one area of Asian Buddhism, sex discrimination is so troublesome that Asian women are organizing to correct it. This is the ordination of Buddhist nuns. The original nuns' order is said to have disappeared after a thousand years, and in Southeast Asian countries there have been no fully ordained nuns for centuries. Because only a company of fully ordained nuns can ordain a nun, the full ordination of nuns cannot take place. Hong Kong, Taiwan, and Korea have surviving nuns' orders, and the nuns offer full ordination to qualified women, but this ordination is not considered valid by the Buddhist establishment in some Southeast Asian countries. As a result, there are about sixty thousand women in the Buddhist tradition, mostly Asian women, who call themselves nuns, wear robes, and live a renunciant's life, but most have not received the full authorization of their tradition. Thus many of the women who have dedicated their entire lives to the Dharma are denied the material support of the sangha, kept from the teachings and instruction they need, and treated like servants and religious nonentities.

Sakyadhita, or Daughters of the Buddha, is an international organization dedicated to the support of Buddhist women, both lay and nuns. They have held several conferences at which nuns and laywomen from various countries and traditions have been able to share information. Included among these women are fully ordained nuns from Hong Kong and Taiwan—where the *bhikshuni* ordination was preserved unbroken—who provide inspiration to nuns suffering in oppressive situations.

In the United States, among Western practitioners, Buddhism has been open to women from the beginning. American women are in Buddhism, doing Buddhism, creating Buddhism. Some choose to work in male-dominated situations; others have moved out of these settings to forge their own paths. No woman should have to give up on Buddhism because she encounters a woman-denigrating situation in a particular Buddhist center. In these settings it is best to trust your instincts. If you feel that this is not a group in which you will be allowed to realize your spiritual potential, leave the group and find a teacher who respects you and your needs, even if you have to do it by mail or travel long distances. The Buddha pointed out that according to our individual capacities we are receptive to particular kinds of teaching. Let yourself find the teachings and the teacher that can help you explore yourself, in a Buddhist setting that acknowledges and respects women.

A Practice to Begin With

In Vipassana settings we do a practice called metta. *This is the lovingkindness meditation. It is meant to soften our ego-edges, release us from our hatred, hurt feelings, and guilt and open our hearts to ourselves and others. A teacher leads this meditation, talking us through it, but it can be practiced by oneself.*

METTA MEDITATION

Sit in a comfortable posture, back straight, eyes closed. Focus on your breath for a time, in order to quiet your mind. Take as much time as you need to calm down.

Now imagine yourself seated in front of you. Look at this woman who is you, her posture, her appearance, her expression, and the feeling you get from her. Be aware of these aspects of yourself, not judging or comparing, just observing yourself.

When you feel ready, open your heart and send lovingkindness to yourself. Shower yourself with love and tenderness and compassionate understanding. Let yourself receive this gift and fully absorb it. Then wish for yourself: May I be free of the hostility and anger I sometimes feel, the antipathy that closes my heart and makes me pull away from other beings or act aggressively toward them.

May I be free from grief, the longing and sorrow for what has changed or no longer exists.

May I be free of disease, ailments of the body and mind that sometimes wrack me.

May I be happy.

Allow yourself to fully receive these wishes and absorb the good feeling that accompanies them.

Now imagine a person who is close to you and whom you love very much, a dear friend or relative, your partner, your child. See this person before you and open your heart to her or him. Send tender love and compassion to this person. Then wish:

May you be free from anger.

May you be free from grief and disease.

May you be happy.

Now choose a person for whom you have neutral feelings. Send lovingkindness to him or her, and wishes for their well-being.

So far this has probably been fairly easy to do, but now we progress to a challenge. Think of a person who is difficult for you, whose very presence plunges you into your most constricted, unloving self. See that person before you. Just look at him or her for a moment, really seeing them. Now do your best to send affection and tenderness to this person. Make the effort to open your heart, even just a little bit, and reach out to this person with love. It may hurt, it may not seem possible, but really try to do this. Now make your wishes for them:

May you be free from anger.

May you shake off your grief.

May you avoid disease.

May you be joyful.

Let yourself fully open to this person and wish him or her well.

Now call forth a person whom you have wronged, someone you treated callously, that you withheld from, that you vented your anger on, that you ridiculed or otherwise disrespected. Place this person before you and look at him or her. Feel the guilt and shame that come naturally from your actions. Now go past these feelings to radiate lovingkindness from your heart to this person. Repair the damage with your love. Wish him or her freedom from hostility, freedom from sorrow and physical or mental illness. Wish that he or she may be happy.

Now imagine a person who has done you wrong, someone who has hurt or humiliated you, whom you find it hard to forgive. Set this person before you and look at him or her, see them really as they are. Now, even though you feel injured and not acknowledged, do your best to send your loving thoughts and feelings to this person. Surround him or her with tender loving care. Make the wishes for this person.

From these very personal encounters now we expand our awareness to all the beings of this neighborhood or country town or city, the people, the dogs and cats, the opossums and raccoons, the bluejays and wrens, and all the other animals and birds that live here. Let your lovingkindness expand to reach out in a great circle and touch all beings in your immediate environment.

Now reach out farther, including the inhabitants of the United States or even the whole continent of North America. Besides human beings and animals, now open to all living beings, trees, flowers, amoebas, rocks, earth itself. Let your heart open so wide that it encompasses this whole great continent and all the beings living on it. Send lovingkindness to all these beings. Wish them freedom from anger, from grief and disease. Wish for their happiness.

Finally, imagine the universe, with planets and stars, extra-terrestrial beings, divine emanations, sun and moon and our own earth. Send your love out to the whole extent of our known and unknown universe. Shower that vastness with your love and compassion.

Now return to yourself, this person who sits here. Once again see her before you, and with all the expansiveness you've just experienced, once again send lovingkindness to yourself. Receive it, and wish for yourself an end to hostility and anger. Wish yourself free of grief. Wish health to your body and mind, and allow happiness to live in you.

This practice will certainly increase your concentration, and it may actually exert a healing effect upon your relations with specific people, helping you to let go of your negative feelings and just see the person for who he or she is, separate from your needs and predilections. Physical healing may also be enhanced by the practice of metta.

But it is in the doing itself that the real benefits occur, for during this time you are reinforcing the most positive qualities in yourself, fully welcoming yourself and embracing the world around you.

IV | *The Teachings from a Woman's Perspective*

The Buddhist teachings present a broad, penetrating, illuminating, and ultimately liberating view of human existence. But on first encounter, a few elements may seem strange or troubling. Certain questions crop up again and again, and women often have particular concerns about some aspects of the teachings.

One dimension that troubles some people is the Buddha's First Noble Truth: that we suffer. In our forward-looking Western culture, where positive thinking dominates, the idea that to be a human being is to suffer may seem negative and repellent. Who would want to subscribe to a belief system that puts suffering at its center! This "truth" may not even seem to hold up, because life contains joy and happiness as well as suffering.

But if we look more closely at what the Buddha meant, we find that the truth of suffering is not a negative, restrictive perception but a way to greater freedom and equanimity in our lives. One scholar translated the Pali term *dukkha*, or suffering, as "the general unsatisfactoriness of life." Suffering is likened to a wheel that rides a little crooked, so that as it turns there is moment-by-moment friction. This kind of suffering includes not only active pain but also a general discontent or uneasiness that we feel, even sometimes in the midst of a happy situation.

You can experience the First Noble Truth by merely sitting still. When you sit to meditate, you arrange myself in a comfortable position, legs crossed, back straight; for a few moments you are at ease, but then your knee starts to hurt. Now you are faced with a decision. Do you hold your position, or move your knee? You move and are comfortable again. But soon you realize a fly has alighted on your face and is walking down your cheek toward your mouth. What to do? You shake your head, and the fly leaves. Ah, comfort again. But now you see in your mind a person who works with you. The two of you are having a conflict at work, and just seeing his face in your imagination awakens a great frustration and anger in you. You struggle to pay attention to your breath. Finally you are comfortable again, but you're worried: you want the comfort to stay, but you know that in a few moments something will change and you'll feel physical or mental or emotional pain again. You may even hear an inner voice that says, "You are not doing this right. You're screwing up again. Can't you ever just *sit still* without making yourself unhappy?"

At a retreat, Ruth Denison looks at us from the front of the room and says, "Here you are with nothing to do but focus on yourself. You don't have to work or tend to other people. This is a comfortable warm room in which we are sitting. In an hour we will go to lunch, which has been cooked for you. Then you'll take a nap. All your needs are provided for here. Why are you unhappy? Why do you suffer?"

And we see that it is the nature of existence as human beings to be plagued by this discontent.

"Yes," you may say, "but there are times in my life when I'm filled with joy, delirious with pleasure, and suffering is far from me." Perhaps, but in those times we may say to ourselves or to others, "I want this moment to last forever," and we know it won't. So in the most ecstatic experience is embedded that tiny seed of pain.

Christianity says we suffer because of "original sin," because Eve gave the apple of awareness of good and evil to Adam to eat. The Buddhist view of suffering, on the other hand, has nothing to do with sin or with a god who punishes us. We suffer simply because we live in a conditioned world in which everything changes all the time. And in this world of ever flowing

An Immigrant's Daughter

A friend of mine grew up in New York with her immigrant parents. Her mother and father had escaped poverty and oppression in Poland to come to the land of freedom and tolerance. They set out to make a life here, prove themselves worthy of being real Americans. So they worked very hard, and they insisted upon a resolutely positive attitude in themselves and in their children. Negative thoughts were not allowed; pain was to be stoically borne and not talked about; sorrow was banished from the house. When this little girl became a woman, she came to the Buddhist teachings, and she was flooded with relief. "At last," she said, "I was given permission to feel the suffering that was really there in our lives."

and transforming phenomena, we want things to be stable and reliable, we have certain ideas of how our life should be, we cling to what we think we have and grieve when it collapses and goes away. We live in the past or the future, almost never arriving here in the present moment. This is dukkha, or suffering.

American culture denies and runs from suffering. Advertising tells us that we can all live like gods, free of care, free of disease and discomfort, laughing in the sunlight as the breeze lifts our hair. Those who conspicuously suffer, like the homeless, the impoverished elderly, the poor, and the mentally ill are to be ignored, because suffering is un-American.

Suffering is just here with us, and rather than run from it or deny it, we can learn to embrace it, to examine it in order to fully experience and know its qualities, and then to let it go. This does not mean that we should seek out personal suffering or cause suffering to others; nor does it mean that we do not act to alleviate pain in others and ourselves. Yet despite all our efforts, still we experience discomfort and pain, worry, anxiety, fear interlaced in the moments of our daily life.

Suffering as a Beginning

The Buddha directed us to turn our attention to the suffering in our lives, as his First Noble Truth, but he did not stop there. He moved on to give three other truths that mark the way out of this suffering.

In the Second Noble Truth, he defined the origin of suffering as our craving and our clinging. We are always desiring more or other, and we cling to what we have, wanting to possess it forever.

There is a Pali word, *tanha*, which means craving. Tanha is what drives the life of the world. Soon after a baby comes out of the womb it makes sucking motions; it wants to eat, to satisfy itself. From then on the human being is always reaching out to acquire, to devour. And once we get something, we want to hold onto it forever. If the baby did not suck, it would die. On the other hand, because the nature of life is the impermanence of everything, even our physical bodies, our craving and clinging cause us pain. There is no way to possess anything indefinitely; our stable, solid world is a fiction; and so we suffer.

Then the Buddha noted that there *can be* an end to suffering, and this insight is known as the Third Noble Truth. The push and pull of our ordinary conditioned existence seems inevitable once we become aware of it, and yet the Buddha said that human beings are capable of escaping this continual disease.

Finally in the Fourth Noble Truth he set out the path that leads to the extinction of suffering, which he called the Noble Eightfold Path. The efforts pursued on this path can be grouped as Wisdom, Morality, and Meditation. One studies and practices in order to arrive at Right Understanding and Right Thought, that is, in order to achieve *Wisdom*. One maintains *Morality* by practicing Right Speech, Right Action, and Right Livelihood. And finally to develop *Meditation*, one follows the Buddha's directions for Right Effort, Right Mindfulness, and Right Concentration.

So the awareness of suffering in our lives, from the slightest itch to the most intense mental or physical anguish, opens the door to a spiritual path that can lead to liberation. The Buddha said:

"Not only the fact of Suffering do I teach
but also the deliverance from it."

Do I Have to Let Go of My "Self"?

You may have heard that the concept of the self is denied in Buddhism. Indeed, the idea of *Anatta*, or "Not-Self," is one of the three great "marks" of Buddhism. The other two are Suffering, which we have just examined, and Impermanence, which is not so hard for Westerners to grasp, for we surely have noticed the continual flux, the building up and decaying and falling away of everything around us. And in our own Greek-inspired philosophical tradition we have this concept, most clearly stated by Heraclitus as "All things change, nothing abides" and "You cannot step into the same river twice."

But the idea of the insubstantiality of the individual self is a harder concept for Westerners to credit or experience. The self is said by Buddhism not to exist at all but simply to be a useful illusion, a persona that allows us to move through the world, go to work, fix the car, and cook dinner. One of the things Buddhist practice is designed to create is a direct experience of the not-self.

Westerners often find this concept threatening, offensive—at the least hard to understand. Those with Christian or Jewish backgrounds may not want to give up the belief in the individual soul. And women, in particular, may react with anger: "Does Buddhism say I'm supposed to get rid of my ego? How can I even consider this when as a woman I need to *build up* my ego!"

Both psychology and feminism emphasize the development of a strong, stable self as a basis for mental health. The conventional socialization of women has served to undermine our sense of ourselves as autonomous, powerful beings, creating in some women a fragile or vulnerable self. Such women often find it difficult to act effectively in the world, protect themselves, and pursue their own ideas and desires. Thus most women try to develop their sense of self, to build up more confidence in the substantiality and strength of who we are.

The Buddhist concept of the not-self *does* threaten our habitual reliance on a stable self, but it leads to perception of a larger reality more reliable than this persona upon which we depend. The Buddhists describe the "self" as a collection of components, made up of many elements and having no coherent reality separate from those elements. In this way, it can be compared to a car. It seems to have solidity, substantial presence, power, perhaps beauty. Yet if we look closer we see that the car is composed of disparate parts—an engine, a muffler, a steering wheel, fenders, upholstery. Suppose we were to disassemble the parts. The car would no longer exist, because it has no inherent existence, only a constructed or conditional one.

In the Buddhist view the same is true of this self we cherish and believe in. And furthermore it is our belief in this self, our identification with it that causes us to suffer. When you look at your self, how stable and consistent is it? Don't we act differently, feel differently, according to conditions? One hour I'm a contented, helpful person; the next I'm a tight-lipped angry woman. "I'm not myself," we say. "I didn't know myself." Could it be that this self we cherish has no reality separate from our moods, that it is nothing but a complex of responses to the conditions we encounter around and inside us? Being mindful of this self can help us identify the habitual behaviors and reactions that enslave us.

Freedom, say the Buddhists, begins with a disidentification from the self. How does that feel? I admit I rarely am able to arrive at a state of balance and equanimity where my self is concerned. I am as identified as the next person with my appearance, my work, my intellectual and physical capacities. But through meditation I have had experiences that placed me in a different relationship to this self, showed me its arbitrary existence, its lack of inherent being.

Obviously we need this self, or persona, to carry out all the duties and experience all the pleasures of ordinary existence. But our level of belief in and identification with this self is a matter for each of us to examine and work with.

If the self does not ultimately exist, what does? Buddhism posits a reality undergirding or encompassing our ordinary reality. This has various names—the Unconditioned, the Great Ground of Being, Big Mind, or even the Great Self. In meditation I am sometimes able to let go of all the busyness of my mind and body, and then I experience a different quality of being—a deep, silent peacefulness, which is expansive and inclusive of all that exists. This I take to be an experience of the Ground of Being. We partake of this. It exists before any creation and after dissolution.

I remember a Zen *gesshin*, or teacher, a German woman who had experienced war and privation. She sat at the front of a crowded room in her gray robe, her shaved head shining slightly in the afternoon light from a window, and her presence radiated a deep serenity, a *sureness* that I certainly did not find in myself, "You are *this*," she said. "There is nothing that can be

A Revelation about the Self

I was privileged to spend six weeks living as a Theravada nun in a nunnery in Sri Lanka. We meditated for many hours each day as part of our routine. In one morning meditation, as the sun began to rise outside our open-air meditation hall, after I had been meditating peacefully for forty-five minutes, I began to be plagued by discomfort in my right knee. It began as a dull ache, then changed to a piercing pain. I determined not to move but to turn my attention fully to the sensations in my knee and examine the qualities of this pain. I was able to do this, no doubt because I had already achieved a strong level of concentration. So I attended to the pulsing of the pain, its searing sharpness, its subtle shifts and changes. In doing this I lost the sense of this leg as being my *leg.*

My knee became simply a play of energy, almost as if it were a molecular flow, a dance. Delight and intense interest flooded me. How fascinating it was that there was no sensation of pain, but only of subtle movement. I continued to observe the sensations for several minutes. Then the thought came, but this is my *knee, and with that identification—that owning of my knee—the* added to you, and nothing can be taken away. You are complete." I could feel that she spoke from her own experience, that she was reporting to us a truth that she knew firsthand. And I felt a relaxation in myself, as if I had been shown the end of striving, of struggling, of trying. Why struggle when we *are already*, each of us, a part of the essential nature of the universe?

Awareness of this deep harmony can provide us with much more real strength and stability than reliance on our usual limited, ever shifting selves. This is why the truth of Anatta or not-self is a liberating insight.

dance of energy solidified and became a piercing pain again. I was suffering, and I understood that my suffering was the result of my identification with the I.

I decided to try to return to that earlier consciousness. Steadfastly I concentrated on the sensations in my leg, going deep inside them, and soon once again I perceived only the movement of atoms. Nothing existed but my attention and that flow of energy. Then I shifted back to the I-consciousness, saying to myself, "my knee," and immediately I suffered extreme pain. As long as I maintained my concentration, I was able to shift back and forth from one way of perceiving to the other.

When the teacher rang her bell to end our meditation session, I knew that never again could I believe in the absolute reality of my self. I really understood that my clinging to it and solidifying it was the root cause of the suffering in my life.

How Does Buddhism Relate to Bodies?

The Buddhist view of the body gives it a central place. The strict Theravada monastic tradition includes meditations in which one views the body in its most down-to-earth, ignoble aspects, as a bag of piss and shit and blood and mucus. There is a classic meditation on a corpse, in which the monk sits before a decaying body for days and watches it disintegrate. We are also told that one Buddhist teacher slept for a year on the bones of his mother. Each of these practices is designed to remind one that the body exists for only a limited time and is subject to the same decay and dissolution as every other form of life. Unlike belief systems that elevate the mind over the body, Buddhism views the body as no less real and valuable than consciousness. As scholar Joanna Macy has written in an unpublished manuscript, "the Buddhist view is process, and no substance—mental, psychic, or supernatural—is aloof from process. No essence is held up as inherently nobler or purer or realer than this bag of decaying flesh. The monk's goal, in reflecting on the body, is to become more mindful of it, not to withdraw from it or to alter it."

The body is one of the major foundations of mindfulness. Vipassana meditation practice, the original practice developed by the Buddha, begins with an examination of the body. And it is considered a great advantage to be born into a human body, as it is believed that humans have a better chance of becoming enlightened than other living beings.

Much Buddhist practice involves attention to and use of the body. Zen sitting posture, for instance, is probably familiar to everyone. You've seen pictures of the shaven-headed monk in black robe, back straight, legs crossed in the lotus position, hands cupped at midriff, eyes lowered. The strong emphasis in Zen on posture, body sensation, and on the breath tends to help the sitter keep her mind focused on the present moment. The following "Zazen Rules" as recorded in this excerpt from *Zen Is Eternal Life* by Roshi Jiyu Kennett, describe in precise detail the Zen sitting posture and attitude:

> Place a round cushion on top of a thick square one on your seat. Some people meditate in the full-lotus position and others in the half-lotus one. In the full-lotus position your right foot is placed upon your left thigh and your left foot is placed upon your right thigh; in the half-lotus position the left foot is placed upon the right thigh and nothing more; do not wear tight clothing. Rest the right hand on the left foot and the left hand in the palm of the right hand with the thumbs touching lightly; sit upright, leaning neither to left nor right, backwards nor forwards. The ears must be in line with the shoulders and the nose in line with the navel; the tongue must be held lightly against the back of the top teeth with the lips and teeth closed. Keep the eyes open, breathe in quickly, settle the body comfortably and breathe out sharply. Sway the body left and right then sit steadily with the legs crossed, neither trying to think nor trying not to think. Just sitting, with no deliberate thought, is the important aspect of Zazen.

In Vipassana and Tibetan Buddhist settings also, body posture in sitting is important, though not as strict as the Zen posture. In Vipassana, if one experiences discomfort or pain in sitting, that can be viewed as an advantage, for it offers a strong sensation on which to focus one's attention, not allowing for drifting. The practice of sitting still, even through discomfort or pain, or "sitting through" the pain, while simply watching it, is an important teaching that can help us step back a bit from the mind-noise of suffering and view our discomfort within the whole context of our sitting.

Some Vipassana teachers conduct a practice called "sweeping," a bringing of attention to every part of the body and examining the sensations there. This practice, if done well, can lead to profound insight. Ruth Denison is a master of this form of meditation. I remember a long meditation focused on the body in which she brought me finally to a perception of my own skeleton and skull, in which I understood its fragility, its transience. In this consciousness I was flooded with love and compassion for the other people in the room, knowing each of us must die, feeling how brief is our time in this life.

In Tibetan Buddhism the beginning training is quite physical. The practitioner performs hundreds of full prostrations each day, while reciting a mantra and visualizing a deity. A full prostration entails bowing, kneeling, lying fully stretched out on the ground, getting up again. This practice is extremely demanding, physically as well as psychologically.

In a Korean Zen center I visited, the female and male monks do 108 bows each day as part of the morning service. These bows entail going down to rest on one's knees and touching one's head to the floor. In my short stay at the monastery, I learned just how strenuous this practice is. That first morning, as everyone around me was bowing easily, I imagined I would have no problem. But after about thirty bows, my legs stiffened to such an extent that I thought it better to simply bow from the waist, standing up. The next day my legs rebelled, I had a charley horse in each thigh, and I could go downstairs only by gripping the banister and lowering myself with excruciating slowness to the next step. (Most bowing in Zen centers is not so athletically challenging. Usually, at the most, nine bows are done.)

Bowing in Zen Buddhism has profound significance. It is first a concentrative practice, engaging the body in movement to help the mind throw off distraction. Then it is an act of reverence to the Buddha or enlightened mind, a physical acknowledgment of the Buddha-nature in each of us. When done with full concentration and total surrender to this action alone, it is as if the person disappears and only the bow is enacted. In that sense it is a giving up of ourselves, letting go of all our small-mind ideas of self and other, of comparisons, judgments, definitions. Suzuki Roshi, a distinguished Zen master, said, "When you forget all your dualistic ideas, everything becomes your teacher, and everything can become the object of worship." Thus in offering up our small selves as we bow, we surrender into the big self where everything is just as it is and everything is to be respected. This is the significance of the bow.

The bowing also expresses the Zen Buddhist vows:

> "Although sentient beings are innumerable, we
>   vow to save them.
> "Although our evil desires are limitless, we vow to
>   be rid of them.
> "Although the teaching is limitless, we vow to learn
>   it all.
> "Although Buddhism is unattainable, we vow to
>   attain it."

Reading these vows, you're probably thinking, "But these are impossible to accomplish!" Indeed they are, but if one's deepest desire is to shed the baggage of self-centeredness, one must make the effort, and in the effort one achieves calmness of mind.

So the bowing expresses one's most profound longing and leads to immersion in the Great Self or All That Is.

The walking meditation described at the end of Part Two is another example of the use of the body to enhance mindfulness of our experience. If you have tried it, you may have felt the benefits of deepened calm and increased peacefulness.

Besides the traditional body practices of sitting, bowing, and walking, some teachers are now using slow yoga- or dance-like movements to help students quiet their minds. Women teachers were the first to employ these practices, sometimes improvising movements, sometimes incorporating Native American or other forms of dance and ritual that demonstrate our connection to the earth and all of nature.

Buddhism is known as the Middle Way. The Buddha in his first encounters with spiritual practice chose the way of austerities and mortification of the body. He went without eating, sat in the forest day and night in all weathers, paid no attention to his clothing or cleanliness. Eventually, after years of these practices, he realized that they would not lead him to liberation. He began to eat and otherwise take care of his body, for he reasoned that a healthy, strong body would be a better vehicle for enlightenment than a starving, weakened physical frame. At the same time he did not allow himself to surrender to luxurious surroundings, sensual pleasures, debauchery. So this path, which avoids the extremes of both self-denial and self-indulgence, came to be known as the Middle Way.

The general Buddhist attitude to the body, then, can be seen in this context. We maintain our health and take care of our bodies, valuing them as the essential "environment" in which spiritual practice can be pursued. It is a path of moderation, of balance and equanimity in worldly life.

What about Sex?

As discussed earlier, we abstain from sexual activity during Buddhist retreats, so that we can focus inward and concentrate on our meditation practice. In ordinary life the situation is different. Sex and procreation are viewed as natural parts of existence. More and more Buddhist centers welcome families and create events including children. A sexual relationship is seen as wholesome when it promotes the well-being of both partners, and when no one is injured or disturbed by it. Particular teachers and sanghas may interpret the precept "to avoid sexual misconduct" differently; for example, they may require that sexual contact be accompanied by commitment. Each of us probably knows what makes sexual behavior unwholesome or destructive for us, and what a mutual, respectful, supportive, passionate, and compassionate sexual relationship would be. Wholesome behavior is choosing at each juncture to opt for the latter.

Many Buddhists look to their sexual relationship as a fertile ground in which to practice lovingkindness and compassion, to learn patience and large-heartedness. They recognize that our primary, committed relationships challenge us to confront our most troublesome tendencies and to act decently and supportively with our partners.

Same-sex relationships are as accepted within Buddhist environments as heterosexual unions. There may be residual homophobia among the participants in any given center, but Buddhist doctrine nowhere condemns homosexuality or lesbianism and therefore offers no basis for a negative view. Buddhist teachers look at the relationship itself, judging it on the basis of its beneficial or unwholesome qualities rather than on the sex of the partners.

What Place Do Emotions Have?

You may have gone to a Buddhist meditation session in which the participants sat stiffly, in silence, where all warmth and emotional response seemed to be forbidden. Indeed, some people choose a spiritual path in the effort to escape unruly emotions, and they seek to suppress, deny, and eradicate their feelings. The result is a robot-like complacency. This can happen in a Buddhist environment, but it is never the ideal.

Buddhism does not ask us to step away from or suppress our emotions. Because we are human beings, we experience anger, greed, sorrow, grief, longing, as well as more pleasant feelings. There is no blame attached to this. When the emotion

An Encounter with Anger

On the Nuns Island in Sri Lanka, all our needs were taken care of. We were housed, fed, counseled. We worked a few hours each day, but the rest of our time was given to meditation and study. There was no electricity on the island and no other residents, no newspapers, no media. It was an extremely peaceful environment. Yet one day I found myself consumed with rage.

It happened like this. We rose each morning at 4:30 A.M., put on our white robes, and made our way up the dark path to the meditation hall. Personally I found 4:30 to be a very early hour. But one day Stacey, an enthusiastic American student, reminded our teacher Ayya Khema that the description she had read of the nunnery specified the waking hour as 4:00 A.M. Could we, asked Stacey, get up at four instead of four-thirty? Ayya Khema was bemused but agreeable. "Yes," she said, "beginning tomorrow we will rise at four A.M."

I was at first annoyed. Why did Stacey have to do that? How could she be so gung-ho! In the meditation hall I sat chewing this over, and as I sat there the annoyance turned to anger, and built and built until it was a fury burning in me. Part of me was sur-

arises in us, we are taught to fully allow its presence and to observe it in order to learn more about its nature. Ideally, we neither feed it nor seek to weaken or stop it, we simply watch it
arise, run its course, and subside.

There is no way for us in meditation and daily life not to feel
our emotions. They spontaneously leap up, in response to the
actions of others and our own thoughts. We have no choice in

> *prised; how could I get so upset over such a ridiculous thing? The*
> *rest of me raged: Isn't 4:30 early enough! My god, it's already the*
> *middle of the night! And now she wants us to get up earlier! Why*
> *did she have to bring this up! There was hatred in me as I ranted*
> *silently about Stacey's youth and foolish exuberance, her pushing*
> *every condition to its ultimate, as I banished her from serious con-*
> *sideration as a rational human being. The rage boiled in me, sear-*
> *ing my insides.*
>
> *This tantrum caused me pain as it built to new levels of ven-*
> *omous animosity toward Stacey. And I watched, astonished, as*
> *I saw how completely I had created this emotion, and how in-*
> *appropriate it felt in this serene monastic setting. But perhaps*
> *it was not inappropriate, for I was shown my own capacity for*
> *anger, which I share with every other human being, and I was*
> *given the opportunity to observe it fully. So I watched my rage*
> *build and sustain itself and finally, slowly, begin to dissipate.*
> *Not until evening had the anger stilled. I felt emotionally*
> *wracked and pushed to my limits by my daylong experience,*
> *but when I went to bed that night I knew I had been given a*
> *profound teaching.*

the matter. But we do have a choice of how to receive and work with these emotions.

The Zen teacher Maurine Stuart told how when her own teacher, an old Japanese master, was happy, he glowed with delight, and when he felt pain, tears came to his eyes. "He was so vividly *in life*, as we all should be," she said. "There is none of that deadness in real Buddhist living."

In meditation halls, sometimes people sit with tears streaming down their faces. When you stop talking and doing, and sit still, everything that is in you has a chance to assert itself. It may be obsessive thinking and planning; it may be the sorrow you never allowed yourself to feel at the death of your brother; it may be a spontaneous happiness at just being alive. All of this is not only allowed but welcomed, because it provides us the opportunity to become mindful, to begin to know ourselves.

What Is the Meaning of Detachment?

The Buddhist concept of "detachment" can sound very male, and very much like not-caring. It is exactly the opposite. It is total caring, total attention to the moment at hand—but without grasping for more.

There is a famous story about a young village woman who became pregnant and did not want to reveal her lover's name, so she told her parents that the father of the child was a monk who lived in a hut outside of town. The parents, enraged, brought the newborn baby to the monk and handed it to him, saying, "Take it, it's yours." The monk took the baby. From then on he had to give up much of the meditation practice he had followed before in order to care for the infant. He raised it, nurturing and tending it with all his powers of attention and compassion. When the child was a few years old, its mother told her parents that she had lied, that the monk was not the father of the child. The parents and the young woman came to the monk's hut and took back the healthy young child. The monk went on with his meditations as before.

This is a model of detachment. The monk entered fully into the life that was given to him. But he was not *attached to the outcome.*

The story may seem strange to us because we are so used to thinking of caring as *holding on*, establishing ownership, and demanding continuity. So much of how we feel about something depends on how it turns out, whether it lasts, whether it develops in the way we think it should. When something passes away, deconstructs, drifts off, we cling to its memory and experience regret. And some of us are addicted to what we call "passion." We imagine passionate living to be those storm-tossed times in which our emotions lift us away from our better judgment.

But the Buddhist view of a full life is passionately attending, each moment, to the task at hand, to the sensations one is experiencing, the relationship one is in with another being—to be fully in the present moment, giving oneself to it completely without thinking of past and future.

How Can I Understand Enlightenment?

Everyone has experienced moments of complete balance and clarity, in which all needs are met, all questions answered. These moments occur in the midst of daily life, sometimes in response to our situation: while swimming or making love, after a good meal, in the woods or at the seashore. In these instants we are connected to that which is most fully human in ourselves; in other words we are linked to our intrinsic or essential nature. So each of us has experienced moments of enlightenment.

Enlightenment is not a magical transcendance of ordinary life but awareness of our unity with the Great Ground of Being. In actual fact we embody and express enlightenment, but most of the time we are so busy striving to get what we do not have that we are unaware of it.

The practices of Buddhism—meditation, compassion, Dharma study, scrutiny of our own actions in the world—provide or create the conditions that can allow our preoccupations to fall away, so that we can experience our unity with the big mind or primal awareness. That experience is only clumsily described in words, because it is deeper than our ordinary consciousness; it transcends the verbal forms we have to describe things. And it arises spontaneously. You cannot make it happen, but you can work to clear out your distractions, open your heart, quiet your mind, so that this deep sense of ultimate peace can be felt in all the atoms of your being.

Meditators and others often ask whether Enlightenment is the only goal in Buddhism. I remember a friend raising her hand to ask a nun-teacher, "What if I just want to be a better person?" One of the major endeavors of Buddhism is right action in the world, doing good instead of evil, being mindful and careful of other people, animals, all beings, even all objects that exist with us in this universe. Most people, like my friend, would agree that this goal is difficult enough to engage us fully. Yet we can realize that this effort is rooted in a larger context that can become known to us and can suffuse our life with a deep serenity. This essence of being is always with us.

Is Compassion a Trap for Women?

Hearing of Buddhism's strong emphasis on compassion—sharing the suffering of others and acting to offer aid—you may find yourself, quite logically, objecting, "Look, as women we've been trained to be compassionate and take care of other people all our lives, and it is this training that causes us to give too much and be taken advantage of! Is Buddhism just telling me once again to be a 'good woman'?"

One major dimension of the female role in every society in the world is caring for others. Despite the recent innovations of feminism, most women are conditioned from birth to provide support: we are taught to give up our own desires and ambitions in order to promote the desires and ambitions of boyfriends and husbands, and our best efforts are given to the nurturance of children. Even most women with jobs or careers are principally responsible for their children. In this life-long endeavor women sometimes feel that they have given away *themselves*, so that they no longer know what they feel or desire.

Many contemporary women have been able to choose a different path, at least for a time. But the expectations of society are so pervasive that we are especially sensitive when the subject of nurturance or service to others arises. We may recoil from the Buddhist emphasis on compassion or at least regard it with distrust.

Some women might advise, since we are so trained in giving to others, that we bypass the training in compassion and focus instead on other elements of the Buddhist path. We might train ourselves in skillful means, for instance, or concentrate on meditation practice.

But the Buddhist concept of compassion is quite different from the continual giving and going outside of oneself that characterizes traditional female behavior. In Buddhist compassion, the person acts from a fullness of being, the motivation coming from herself, not from the requirements or expectations of others. It is a natural flow that does not diminish the giver.

Wisdom and compassion are the two most crucial dimensions of Buddhism; they express a deep, universal consciousness and constantly inform each other. Wisdom needs compassion in order to soften its piercing insight; compassion needs wisdom to guide its expression. Compassion arises from the Buddhist awareness that we are all interconnected, we are all part of the Great Ground of Being, and as such we strive to promote the comfort and happiness of all beings.

Significantly, for us as women, we begin with ourselves. The first movement of the meditation to promote compassion is to turn inward and give to *ourselves* the love, the understanding, and forgiveness that can make us whole. The compassion for others comes then from this strong, fulfilled sense of oneself.

And Buddhist compassion is different in another way from our conventional Western idea of mercy. The impulse to help others may look like Christian charity, but it differs in a crucial respect. A distinguished Tibetan teacher described compassion as simply doing what is appropriate in the present moment.

A Brief Encounter

One day a friend was passing a neighborhood bookstore and stopped to look at the marked-down books in bins on the sidewalk. Next to her stood a small boy, shabbily dressed, who was fingering a children's book. My friend became intrigued with his look of absorption and desire as he leafed throught the pages and stared at the pictures.

"You like that book?" she asked.

He glanced up at her. "Yeah."

"Going to buy it?"

"I don't have any money."

My friend saw what needed to happen.

"Let's go inside," she said. And the boy followed her, bringing the coveted volume.

"How much?" she asked at the counter, and paid the price.

Back out on the sidewalk, the boy went one direction, clutching his book, his face radiant. My friend went the other way to continue her errands. There were no thank-you's. The encounter had happened quickly and was over.

When my friend told me about this incident, she described it as a seamless part of her actions that day, remarkable only in her recognition that most days she is not able to act so spontaneously.

For instance, you are walking down the sidewalk when the man in front of you trips and falls. You step forward and help him up, not because you see him as unfortunate or pity him but simply because it is the action that is called for. In responding to this small crisis, you did not, for instance, stop to wonder, "Should I intrude on this man's privacy? He doesn't know me, he might not want to be touched by a stranger," or on the other hand, stop yourself by thinking, "Oh, no, if I help this guy I'm liable to get involved in some drama that'll take my time and energy," or "He looks a bit scuzzy, he might have lice, or even TB, or AIDS; I could catch something if I touch him." All of these very ordinary human responses serve to lift you out of this moment of your life and place you in previous experience or what you read in the newspaper last week or your habit of worrying about things. If you could be truly engaged in this moment you might react spontaneously, step forward, and help the man up.

Buddhist compassion is not the doing of good to someone who is less than oneself but is a response to the interconnections in the great net of being that supports us all. In his book *Coming Home*, scholar and spiritual teacher Lex Hixon describes it as "unhesitating, unpremeditated solidarity with fellow beings. . . . This loving compassion is ecstatic, free from rational calculation concerning how much help one might realistically be able to give . . . it gives the gift of itself. . . . There is no help more far-reaching, practical, or profound." And in no way does this gesture or stance diminish the giver; rather, it enriches us moment by moment in our lives.

Perhaps as women we need to become very conscious of our

responses to people and our actions toward them, in order to be able to distinguish between this wholehearted impulse, which comes from our strength, and the knee-jerk response of duty and conditioning. To liberate oneself from the latter and open to the former could be a profoundly transformative experience.

A Practice to Begin With

The teachings that my own teacher transmits always begin with the body, for the Body is one of the Four Foundations of Mindfulness. (The others are the Feelings, the Mind, and the Contents of Mind.) By contemplating my own physical being I may develop powers of concentration and focus. I will become familiar with a major component of my present reality, which is my own flesh and bones. The body is our container, our vehicle, seat of everything we know: it is always available to us, palpable and present. And in contemplating it, if I am able to stay attentive and let myself contact my body, I may come to an experience of one of the great truths of embodied existence: for I may notice that everything is moving and changing, that my physical being partakes of the great flow of phenomena that we call life.

The practice called "sweeping" that I mentioned earlier helps us connect with our bodies. We set out to "sweep" or travel with our consciousness through all the parts of the body, to penetrate into each area to experience how it feels. This can be done in the space of a minute or two, just touching each part of the body with the mind. Or it may be a meticulous examination that can take much longer. Ruth Denison sometimes leads sweeps that are so precise that one lingers for minutes at a time in the places in our body where we hold the most tension or experience the most stress, examining the sensations in that area until we have experienced them in all their subtlety, and only then moving on to other parts. These sweeps sometimes take up a full hour.

You may do the exercise that follows at your own pace, given the time you have and your willingness to focus on your body. For people who habitually live in their minds, whose approach to the world is relentlessly cerebral, this exercise can offer an opportunity to enter a grounded, relaxed experience of one's physical being. At first this may be difficult or even scary. Feelings may come up, old experiences may surface. Just let the feelings move through you and return to the physical sensations.

SWEEPING MEDITATION

Sit in your meditation posture and close your eyes. Be aware of your whole body as it sits, letting your mind go over the front, back, and sides of your body.

Now go to the top of your head. Move around your skull, noting its bone structure. Experience any form of aliveness there that you can. Focus on the eye sockets, those circles of hard bone; the cheeks, flesh, and bone. Now go to the forehead—that wide expanse—and the sensitive temples. What are the sensations that you notice in your forehead? Sense life there in the line of your eyebrows. (As you do this, relax in your thighs and chest.) Now be aware of your mouth, your throat. Clench your teeth and feel that pressure. Move to your eyeballs, feel their shape inside your head. Remember the other sense organs in your head: the nose, tongue, ears, brain. Experience the physical base of your awareness.

Be aware of your ears, their outer shape and their inner shape. Realize that they regulate both your hearing and your whole body's balance. Go to your tongue, and experience how it lies in your mouth, available for your perception. Press your tongue against the roof of your mouth and notice the sensations there.

Now scrunch up your face, pulling everything toward the center. Feel these strong sensations. Hold it, then let it go, and experience your relaxed face.

Remember that everything in your body is offered for the light of your awareness.

Let your awareness travel down your neck to your shoulders and chest. Note the shape of the breastbone. Connect to the sensations there. Let your right shoulder move, the elbow coming up, and feel how this opens the chest. Now lift your left shoulder. Be the authentic witness to the sensations as you let both arms relax and return to your sides.

Now slowly travel down the right arm from the shoulder to the elbow, the elbow to the hand. Stay with your hand, in an attitude of allowing. Notice all of the sensations there. And notice your mind witnessing these sensations. Now move through the fingers of your right hand into your left hand. Move up to left wrist, elbow, until you come to your left shoulder, noticing all sensations.

Go to the front of your chest, noticing the outline of your chest in your mind. Move to your back, feeling its aliveness. Move from the shoulder blades down to the waistline, being aware of the spinal column that allows you to sit upright.

In this plain, nonreactive meeting of mind with flesh, tensions will be released.

Move into the lower back, to the base of the spine, and feel the sensations there.

Go to the left hip. Make a movement here as an invitation to the mind. Now move your right hip. Feel the effect in your abdomen.This is the foundation of your sitting body—hips, buttocks, pelvis. Feel how you are grounded and supported here.

Notice where the leg connects into the hip socket. Let go, slowly, at this point. Now move into the columns of the thighs, notice their width and shape. They form part of the base of our sitting. The pelvis is nested in the hips and the beginnings of the thighs. Travel gently through this region, feel the vibrations here, the temperature, all the bodily sensations.

Pull your lower belly in against your spine. Hold this, noting how it pushes against your lower back.

Move through this region intently, with ease. Open to your lower back, feel the aliveness of the hips. Notice that the weight from your torso rests here. Feel the touch with the floor. Notice yourself in this perceptive alertness.

Now move down your thighs to your knees, to the shin and calf, to the ankles. Go down both legs at once, witnessing life here. Experience yourself in your feet, the upper part of your feet and then the soles. Let awareness of the toes come to you. Envision them. Feel their aliveness.

This ends your full-body sweep.

Now, having experienced your body slowly, it is good to make a few quick sweeps.

Move like a cloud of awareness, penetrative and soft, from

the top of your head down. Sweep rapidly down to your feet, being cognizant of the interior of your body. Do this several times, like a gentle breeze. Realize your mind moving through your body.

Open your awareness to your whole body at once. Notice that its sensations are always changing. Let the body reveal itself in its true nature, with no solidness. All is changing all the time.

Let it change in your loving awareness.

Sweeping requires concentration. You might want to speak these directions into a tape recorder, so that you can play them back to yourself when you're sitting. In this way you can be guided by an outside voice and brought back to attentiveness if your mind wanders.

Try to stay with the directions so that you can move gently through your whole body.

In the fast sweeps, people have discovered various helpful devices. For instance, one meditator imagines a large brush that moves down her body, its soft bristles touching every part. Another woman visualizes a light that penetrates and illuminates each area of the body as it moves down. Experiment until you find what works best for you.

Sweeping can give us a sense of being firmly grounded in our own aliveness. The process, if we give it our best effort and attention, can be both illuminating and reassuring, for it reminds us that we are part of all the living processes that constitute our world.

V   *A Woman on the Path*

The course of any one woman's life may or may not shine a light on your own choices and challenges. But reading about other women's efforts and experiences on their spiritual paths has encouraged and informed me. So in this final section of the book, I want to give a sense of the movement of my own life, particularly the development of my original practice, and the other spiritual practices and perceptions I have integrated into it.

My Own Trajectory

Although I have never gone through a formal initiation into any sect or order, except temporarily on the Nuns Island, Buddhism determines my outlook and offers me ways to cope with my life. While I had done other spiritual study and some practice, it was not until I was forty years old that I discovered Buddhist meditation. For the first three years of Vipassana practice and Abhidharma (the "higher" teachings) study, I did not call myself a Buddhist, but I eventually realized that Buddhist ideas and practices had become part of my everyday existence and were crucially important to me. And so I began to think of myself as a Buddhist.

I have been a writer since childhood, having begun writing stories at about the age of ten. I knew then that writing would be my vocation, and nothing, no job or other activity, has deflected me from that course. Writing fiction was my first path. And while I worked at many secretarial and other menial jobs during my first decade out of college, in the early 1970s I decided to make the leap and earn my living as a writer, teacher of writing, and writing consultant. For the last twenty-five years that is what I've done, publishing three books of nonfiction and two of short stories, teaching many workshops, and coaching other women (and a few men) in their own writing.

One could view the serious practice of writing as a good preparation for meditation practice. You must sit still for hours at a time, which I learned to do. You have to make use of your own material, trusting what comes up in you as valuable grist for the mill; in this process I developed the habit of turning inward. And I know how to be solitary, while traveling out with my thoughts into imagined worlds. Writing and meditation are the two activities in my life that I *must do* in order to feel centered and satisfied.

In the early 1970s, long before I began to meditate, the women's liberation movement gripped my imagination. I left husband, home, and job to plunge into the political work that we thought would transform the world. My coming together with other women in San Francisco to fight the oppression and abuse of women and to promote women's welfare can only be described as a spiritual shift inside myself. It began with the perception that, as a woman, I shared the fate of all women, so that my action in support of women's fair wages or childcare or the end of rape was action in support of myself.

The ego boundary that had kept me thinking of myself as separate and not subject to oppression broke down, and I recognized that I was part of that vast group of human beings called women. I turned toward women as life and sexual partners. Our lives were dedicated to demonstrating for women's rights, writing and publishing on women's issues, raising children communally, and literally putting our bodies between a woman and any man who was attacking her. Occasionally we kept twenty-four-hour vigils at the homes of women whose male lovers or husbands had threatened them. It was a demanding and enlightening time; we were filled with a sense of deep purpose.

My spiritual training had begun in the Midwest, as a child in the Methodist Church. When I came to young adulthood, I became an agnostic who occasionally read books by spiritual masters such as Ramakrishna and Vivekenanda, Eliphas Levi, Gurdjieff, and Seth. I taught myself yoga by following the directions in a book. But during the 1970s, while working in the women's liberation movement, I gave up all interest in what is conventionally known as "spirituality."

Then, in the early 1980s I was introduced to Buddhist meditation practice, and established a connection with Ruth Denison as a teacher and with her Dhamma Dena center in the Mojave Desert as my spiritual home. In Berkeley where I then lived, I studied the teachings of Buddhism at a Tibetan Buddhist center. Periodically I went with my partner to a Zen monastery to meditate.

Buddhism began to inform my thinking.

Each morning I sat on a pillow in the living room of the house I shared with other people, before the white plaster wall, paying attention to my breath, trying not to hear the radio nattering in the kitchen. Soon I moved to an apartment by myself in Oakland. I acquired a zafu (meditation cushion) and a bell with which to begin and end my meditation. I created a small altar from concrete blocks and a board covered with a blue-patterned cloth. On it I put the bell, two candles, and an incense holder.

In the morning before I went into my study to write, I sat before this altar, lit the candles and a long stick of subtle Japanese incense. Then I did the practices Ruth Denison had taught me: watching my breath, sweeping in my body. Over the weeks and months of effort I could feel the practices begin to deepen and take hold in me; my efforts led more reliably to states of peacefulness. At other times my mind took to the trees and I was terminally distracted, but I went on. And when I opened my eyes and rang the little bell, I felt I had grounded myself in each new day.

As my partner was studying and meditating on retreats with me, I had ample opportunity to examine and discuss Buddhist concepts with her and to test the precepts in my daily life. Often we would analyze a real-life situation in relation to the Buddhist guidelines we were learning and examine our own behavior on the basis of our concept of Right Action. Sometimes we

would set ourselves a task, such as, "Today I will not take anything that is not given me," and the next day we would talk
about our experiences as we had tried scrupulously to follow
that precept. Another day we might vow to utter only Right
Speech, speaking only when necessary, not saying anything
that might cause suffering to others. After our classes at the Tibetan Buddhist Center we compared our notes and went over
difficult points.

In meditation I sometimes challenged myself. I remember
a particular instance in which my lover had expressed romantic
interest in another person. I decided to see whether I could in-
voke the quality of *muditha*, or "sympathetic joy," in relation
to her and the person she desired. Muditha means taking pleasure in the pleasure of others. So I imagined my lover and this
other person making love, and I attempted to feel and send to
them my own joy at how much pleasure they were experiencing. As you can imagine, I usually suffered pangs of jealousy
instead of joy, but sometimes I could almost reach the open
appreciation of these people's pleasure without my own ego-
needs interfering.

This spiritual partnership helped me a great deal. My partner's perceptions often moved my own understanding further,
and her steadiness in practice supported me through the hard
times when I sat before my altar distracted and listless.

Later, with other women, my partner and I created a
Women's Sangha in the San Francisco East Bay and began to sit
regularly with these women.

In 1983 my partner and I joined the Livermore Action
Group to protest the production of nuclear weapons by the

Lawrence Livermore Laboratories, an institution run by the University of California. With our small affinity group, which included some men, some young people, and a woman in her seventies, we meditated before going out to Livermore to confront the grim university police. I spent time in jail for my protest activities, and while there I tried to tap into my beginning spiritual practice in order to tolerate jail conditions with as much equanimity and compassion as possible.

At the same time the women's spirituality movement was beginning in the Bay Area. Starhawk and Zsuzsanna Budapest offered celebrations of women's ancient wisdom—Wiccan (the ancient tradition of witchcraft) trainings, spiral dances, circles to "raise energy." Scholars such as Carol Christ, Charlene Spretnak, Merlin Stone, and Hallie Iglehart were opening our eyes about the nature of ancient goddess cultures. While I was researching and writing a big book on women's participation in Buddhist practice in the United States, I was also attending Wiccan or women's spirituality gatherings.

Through the work of the archeologist Marija Gimbutas, I learned about an ancient matristic culture in which the Goddess had been worshipped, and in which women had exercised equal or greater power than men. The images of goddesses or other transcendant female figures helped me envision spirituality and divine power in female terms. And the view of the European witches in the Middle Ages as healers, midwives, and Wise Women rather than doers of evil provided me with a model of shamanistic, earth-centered female efficacy. It also threw into sharp relief the abomination of the European Inquisition in which most of these wise women were murdered.

While I attended and still do attend women's spirituality gatherings and events, Buddhist meditation provides my central practice and view of the world. I celebrate goddess-energy in all of us and am fascinated by the various forms of the goddess. On my altar stands a many-armed statue of Kwan Yin and a photograph of a painting of the Hindu goddess MahaLakshmi. On the wall of my study hangs a Tibetan thanka representing Green Tara. Sometimes I chant to these female beings; sometimes I visualize them and ask them for help in my daily life. They represent my deeper, larger self.

For several years I offered a workshop entitled Writing Your Spiritual Journey, in which I structured each session around a goddess—the fierce Hindu goddess Durga; Mahuika, an oceanic fire goddess; the Native American Spider Woman; the European Hecate; and others. I used guided meditation and writing to help women find and express the particular qualities that these goddesses awakened in them. These workshops were monthly daylong sessions that had the feel of a retreat, a time set aside to be fully with oneself and go inward.

In 1987, I went with my partner to live for a short time as a Theravada nun on Parappuduwa Nuns Island in Sri Lanka. I did not imagine that I would want to take the robes and assume the permanent identity of a female monastic, but I wanted to experience the cloistered life. In Theravada Buddhism one can enter a monastery for brief periods of time and then return to the world. This life appealed to me in its simplicity, peacefulness, and the depth of practice that is possible in a setting without external distractions. My six weeks on the island yielded rich insights.

I also learned from reading, for on the island I had time to study. In researching and writing *Turning the Wheel*, I had become fascinated with the role of religion and spirituality in society. During our rest periods, I found myself reading the Buddhist books in the nunnery library, as well as economic tomes on the Third World; and I determined that when I returned to the United States I wanted to study religion in some sort of formal setting.

Back in Oakland that next fall, I enrolled in a master of arts program at the Graduate Theological Union. The GTU is a collection of Christian seminaries in which most students earn a Master of Divinity in order to become ministers or priests, but a few study for the Master of Arts degree. My two years at the GTU plunged me into a spiritual-intellectual community in which I met many Christian women who were passionate feminists and brave innovators on women's behalf. Some Catholic nuns challenged all stereotypes with their sophistication and commitment to social change. Some of these Christian women have become my fast friends and collaborators in our spiritual quest. While there I taught a class on Women and Buddhism, bringing my own Buddhist perspective into this Christian environment.

My intention had been to study sexuality and sensuality in religion. I soon found that I wanted to go back in history before the establishment of the present-day world religions of Judaism, Christianity, Buddhism, and Islam to the time of the early matristic societies. I began to research the figure of the temple priestess or "holy prostitute" as an example of female spiritual/sexual agency and power.

I also enrolled in a class given in the Berkeley community by a teacher named Vicki Noble. The course was called "Female Shamanic Training." In this weekly four-hour class, Vicki, who is a healer/shaman, cocreator of the Motherpeace Tarot deck, veteran of much Tibetan Buddhist practice, and author of several books on the healing arts, introduced us to the tools of shamanic work. We studied the ancient divination system of Tarot, did astrology, learned to work with guided meditation and trance states, called upon goddess energy, read a long list of more or less esoteric books, did dream work. In the spring, we presented a festival of healing arts in a public park to bring our work out into the community.

I confess that I can never remember astrological data or fully take on any of the systems that many women find so helpful. But Vicki's class immersed me more deeply in the broad stream of female wisdom and mutual support and brought me closer to goddesses and other female power-figures.

During my years of intensive study at GTU, I maintained my meditation practice, relying on my almost daily sitting to stabilize me in the heady worlds of academia and female shamanism. My Buddhist path had not been wholly without difficulties over the years. Specifically, in the early 1980s, revelations of sexual abuse by male Buddhist teachers troubled me deeply. Not only did I know the suffering of the women involved and their communities, but several of the teachers who had taken sexual advantage of their female students were men whose books I had read, whose teachings transmitted the essence of Buddhism in inspired and translucent language. I cannot reconcile these men's high level of spiritual attainment with their propensity to use female students for their own sexual pleasure. My only comfort is the recent willingness of sanghas to confront these perpetrators. The problem of sexual power abuse, of course, is not limited to Buddhism, but for it to happen within the powerful, delicate relationship of a student to a Buddhist teacher was and is profoundly shocking. I continue trying to understand how this outrage can occur and struggle to maintain a spacious, compassionate attitude toward all concerned.

In the griefs and traumas of my own life, my Buddhist practice has been a strong underpinning. My understanding of impermanence sustained me in the deaths of both my parents. As much as I mourned their passing, I also felt its rightness. I remember one day after the death of my mother, while driving in the car, suddenly I had a vision of ocean waves. Each wave swelled, rose, crested, curled over, fell and disappeared; even as the next wave rose behind it to crest and fall, and the next, and the next. Each wave seemed a generation of human beings. I saw my parents' wave rise high and foam, exist in its full power and completion, then fall away; and felt myself lifted on the next wave. That movement felt as it should be. Something let go in me as I surrendered to this great cycle of energy.

In the 1990s, I found myself drawn to the United Nations Fourth World Conference on Women and its parallel Nongovernmental Forum, which were held in Beijing and Huairou, respectively. A year before the conference I decided to go; the chance to attend that gathering and communicate with women from all over the world would be a culmination to the feminist work I'd been doing for years. I also perceived a sort of stagna-

tion in the U.S. feminist movement, a drift away from the basic
survival issues that concern most women in the world, and I
wanted and needed to hear the voices of women from Africa,
Asia, South America, the Middle East, and Europe to achieve a
perspective greater than our U.S.-centered view.

But I wanted to go as a spiritual-political person, not the
more narrowly political woman I had once been. So I joined
with the Center for Women and Religion at the Graduate
Theological Union, whose delegation soon grew to twenty-
eight women. We prepared for nearly a year before the conference, learning about the conditions of women worldwide. I
wanted to support the Tibetan women in exile, my Buddhist
sisters, in their attempt to bring the issue of China's cruel occu-
pation of Tibet to the conference. I became the liaison between
the Tibetan women and the Center for Women and Religion;
many CWR women pledged to provide support for the Tibetan
women at the conference.

We prepared two presentations. In the first, called "Celebrating Womanspirit," we used symbols (to bypass the language barrier) of women's consciousness of spirituality, such
as a tree, a lotus blossom, an iris, a phoenix, and encouraged
women to discuss how the symbols reflected their own lives
and work in their communities. Our second presentation fea-
tured Lesbians involved in the Catholic, Protestant, Quaker,
Jewish, and independent traditions (I was the token Buddhist),
speaking of how Lesbians are viewed and treated within their
religious establishments in the United States.

Outside the conference I wanted to visit the Chinese home
of the celestial bodhisattva Kwan Yin. She is found most

strongly on a little island in the Yellow Sea off Shanghai. Called Putuo Shan or "Sacred Mountain," the island had been for centuries the central pilgrimage place for the worship of Kwan Yin. At one time there had been more than four hundred temples on the island, all dedicated to this goddess, and she was said to appear there at times to the more sincere pilgrims. I determined to spend time on Putuo Shan and persuaded a Chinese-American friend of mine, who is a psychic and a devotee of Kwan Yin, to accompany me.

One intention I took to the Nongovernmental Forum was to seek out the spirituality in the gatherings of women I would encounter there. I knew that these twenty-six thousand women were the most committed activists involved in social change and development work in their countries. Many were sophisticated in world governmental issues and the political realities that drive governments, far beyond my own consciousness. In the intensely focused political atmosphere I expected to find at the conference, would I sense a spiritual ground or thread?

The NGO Conference turned out to be immensely inspiring and life-changing. We stood behind the Tibetan women in the rain as they lodged a silent protest against the rape of their country by the Chinese and felt the weight of the 1.2 *billion* Chinese people pushing against these nine brave Tibetan women. We gave our "Celebrating Womanspirit" workshop, which was enthusiastically received. The second workshop, on Lesbian participation in religious life in the United States, drew a large curious crowd, including a Chinese security agent who filmed our every word and gesture.

I felt spirituality particularly in women's willingness to explore painful issues together, to go past their own opinions to understand the perspectives of other women, but also in the song and music, the artwork, the dancing that was interspersed with the political sessions, and in the greathearted inclusiveness that I found everywhere. I experienced women from all the major regions of the world speaking their truth, often naming the patriarchy as our enemy, expressing their love for and trust in women.

Visiting Putuo Shan presented a more difficult challenge. Most of its temples had been destroyed by the young communists of the Cultural Revolution. The island had since become a popular destination for Chinese tourists from the mainland, Taiwan, Hong Kong, and the Phillipines; a million arrived each year by boat to lie on the beaches, eat in the fish restaurants, and visit the few remaining temples, which are kept almost as museums. My friend and I opened ourselves to feel Kwan Yin's presence there, and we did feel her, but our efforts to communicate with the monks and nuns in the temples were frustrated, and we were continually surrounded by noisy tourists. We did observe some sincere pilgrims who had come to chant and offer incense and candles at the temples, but they constituted a tiny minority of the people there. We left with the recognition that we could find Kwan Yin in our own hearts and did not need to seek her in the external world.

Greatly energized by the NGO Forum, I returned to Oakland determined to engage once again in active political work. Highland Hospital, the county hospital in Oakland, was and is threatened with closure. This facility serves the needs of the poor and disenfranchised; its closure would impose extreme suffering on thousands of people. I decided that my energies would be best spent in joining the community support group that was working to save Highland Hospital.

But fate does not recognize our agendas. As a friend of mine quipped, "How do you make the Goddess laugh? You tell her your plans."

Just a month after returning from China, in October 1995, I was diagnosed with colon cancer. A week later I underwent surgery. And as I write this I have just finished a six-month course of chemotherapy, and continue with alternative therapies. Healing from cancer is a substantial project that I must manage each day. Ironically, because I had no health insurance at that time, I had to go to Highland Hospital for surgery and further treatment. So instead of rooting for Highland from the outside, I experienced it from the inside; and I went to its crowded wards every week to receive the chemotherapy that may prevent the recurrence of my cancer.

This latest unplanned and unwelcome adventure is a spiritual path in which I am surrounded by a large network of loving friends. I call on my years of Buddhist practice to keep me fully engaged in each moment of this cancer practice. On my altar now are the pictures of some people who were deep Buddhist teachers, like Maurine Stuart of the Cambridge Buddhist Association and Lex Hixon, independent scholar and writer, both of whom are now dead of cancer. They speak to me, offering wisdom and support.

I'm doing fine.

This year I become sixty years old. I have no idea what the future will bring. I hope to be able to write the books I have planned and to continue my practice of meditation, to live actively and joyfully, and be of use to others. If this story of some of my experiences so far has helped you to see your own life with a clearer eye, I am grateful.

Final Practice

To end the narrative part of this book, I offer a guided meditation based on the lotus flower and on the goddess Tara. The lotus is a potent image in Buddhism, its blossom symbolizing spiritual attainment or perfection. In Tantric Buddhism the lotus represents the vulva or female genitalia. In the Pure Land, the buddha is said to sit on a lotus floating on a clear lake. Buddhas and bodhisattvas are often depicted sitting in meditation on giant lotus blossoms. We might think of the lotus as a symbol of the endless generative power of the universe, its beauty drawn from the mud of experience and struggle, exploding in the exquisite beauty of the completely opened blossom.

MEDITATION

Sit in a comfortable position and close your eyes. Be aware of your body, its weight on the chair or meditation cushion, the position of your torso, arms, legs. Make a short inventory of your body. How does it feel? If there are pains or discomforts, simply be aware of them for a few moments and then pass on.

Now bring your attention to your breath. Stay with it a short while, following the passage of air into your nostrils and out again, or the lifting and falling of your belly, until your body and mind have calmed.

Imagine yourself as a lotus root. You are buried deep in the mud at the bottom of a pond. Down here all is dark, fecund, dirty, rich, decaying. Here are the difficult places in your life, your failures, your mistakes. And the profound nurturing mulch that feeds you. Feel this surrounding you. Take in this richness and fertility.

Sense the incorporation of the mud and manure into your stem, which pushes up through the muddy water of the pond bottom. Feel the strength of this stem, nourished by the rich thick mud, as it curves gracefully up through the dark water.

As you push upward, notice that the water becomes more clear until, near the surface, it is perfectly transparent and flooded with light.

Push up out of the water with the lotus bud that has developed on your stem. It is closed, holding all the power and fertility of the pond bottom from which it came.

Slowly the bud opens. Like the flower of your vagina it unfurls petal by petal, moist, dewy, fresh. Each creamy petal is an aspect of yourself that is auspicious and life-producing.

Just watch each petal slowly open, recognize and appreciate the quality it represents, the richness you hold inside yourself and express outwardly.

At the same time stay connected to the mud from which this marvel continuously arises.

Celebrate the fully opened lotus blossom, which expresses your own spiritual opening.

Now see that sitting on the lotus is a beautiful woman. This is the goddess Tara, in her form as Tara the Victorious. She sits in meditation posture upon the lotus. A white goose sits at her feet. A clear moon-disc lies next to the goose. Tara has four arms. One set of arms she holds above her head, hands crossed in the gesture of Joy. In her other set of arms, her right hand, open-palmed, reaches out to bring you whatever you desire; her left hand holds a book balanced on a blue lotus.

Tara is nude from the waist up, clothed only in a billowing scarf that curls out around her shoulders and arms, and an elaborate jewelled headdress. She is called the "Spreader of Great Bliss." Now she picks up the moon-disc, like a clear round lake, and with this disc she sends rays of glorious light to dissolve the torments of our secret fears and failings.

Let yourself receive the light from Tara's moon-disc. Let it penetrate your being and drive out all self-hatred, all the nasty little demons that pick at you.

Feel her vigor, her authority, her wide, deep vision as your own. And let her animate your heart with the Great Joy that is her special gift.

Rest in this power and joy, holding the picture of Tara in your consciousness. Now feel her come closer and closer until she merges with you, until your body becomes hers, your mind and heart Tara's.

Stay with this transformation as long as you like, feeling the expansion, the deep peace that reside in it.

Finally Tara moves away from you. You see her again sitting on her lotus blossom, holding her moon-disc flooded with light. She becomes smaller and smaller as she moves into the distance. At last she is a tiny figure, a point, and then she is gone.

Stay for a time in contemplation of the beautiful empty space that is left.

When you are ready, return into the consciousness of your body in its sitting posture. And concentrate on your breath.

Vow to experience this lotus consciousness in your life, to act from your strength and joy in all your dealings. Realize that you can evoke the image of Tara and the lotus anytime you desire and receive their benefits.

Let yourself view the lotus as a depiction of the complexity and possibilities of our inner selves and see Tara as the outward manifestation of your own power, serenity, and capacity for happiness.

May this meditation be helpful to you.

To end, I offer the merit of the content of this book to the benefit of all beings in all worlds. May they be happy. And may all, without exception, attain the qualities of their intrinsic Buddha nature.

Resources

Directory of Women Teachers

NOTE: *This directory is necessarily incomplete, as there are hundreds of women teachers of Dharma in the United States, many of whose names and activities I do not know. I apologize to them for their non-inclusion, and I urge the reader to call the Buddhist centers listed to see if they have women teachers and to look in the phone book for listings under Buddhism, Zen, Dharma, and Tibetan.*

EASTERN UNITED STATES

Sunyana Graef
Vermont Zen Center
P.O. Box 880
Shelburne, VT 05482
(802) 985-9746
Fax (802) 985-2668

Sunyana Graef has studied and practiced Zen since 1969 as a disciple of Philip Kapleau Roshi. She was ordained and began teaching in 1986. Her Vermont zen center offers sesshins (seven-day meditation retreats) and other meditation opportunities. At the center they strive to have open communication through study groups where people can express themselves, and sangha meetings where consensus decisions are made. Sunyana is married and has two daughters. Besides her work in Vermont, she also teaches at the Toronto Zen Center and Casa Zen in Costa Rica.

Judith Lief
Yonkers, New York
(914) 965-2682

Judith Lief trained extensively in the Vajradhatu tradition with Chogyam Trungpa and headed the Naropa Institute in Boulder, Colorado, for some years. Now, through Vajradhatu/Shambhala International, she teaches meditation at Vajradhatu centers in various locations in the United States and Europe.

Toni Packer
Springwater Center for Meditative Inquiry
7179 Mill Street
Springwater, NY 14560
(716) 669-2141

German-born Toni Packer trained in the Zen tradition at the Rochester Zen Center for many years but broke away from the hierarchy and from all forms of religious ritual in 1981. Inspired by the work of Krishnamurti, she encourages a method of direct discovery of our undivided wholeness, emphasizing the difference between thinking and being. She is director of Springwater Center. Once a year she travels to Northern California to lead a retreat. Her books include *The Work of This Moment* and *The Light of Discovery*.

Barbara Rhodes
Providence Zen Center
99 Pound Road
Cumberland, RI 02864
(401) 658-1464

Trained in the Korean Zen tradition, Barbara Rhodes received transmission as a Zen Master from Korean master Seung Sahn in 1992. She leads retreats and gives talks at centers around the world. Mother of a grown daughter, she earns her living as a nurse.

Sharon Salzberg
Insight Meditation Society
Pleasant Street
Barre, MA 01005
(508) 355-4378

Sharon Salzberg has been practicing and studying in a variety of Buddhist traditions since 1970. She has trained with teachers from many countries, including India, Burma, Nepal, Bhutan, and Tibet. Since 1974, Sharon has been leading retreats worldwide. She teaches both intensive awareness practice and the profound cultivation of lovingkindness and compassion. Sharon is cofounder and guiding teacher of the Insight Meditation Society, devoted to offering meditation training in silent retreats of various lengths. She is also a cofounder of the Barre Center for Buddhist Studies, a center that focuses on the integration of the Buddhist teachings into the modern world. She is the author of *Loving Kindness: the Revolutionary Art of Happiness*.

Arinna Weisman
27 Brookwood Drive
Florence, MA 01060

Arinna Weisman trained with Ruth Denison and teaches in the Vipassana tradition. She teaches retreats for gays and lesbians, and is interested
in integrating political and spiritual activities. Her retreats take place in
Massachusetts, at the Spirit Rock Meditation Center in California, and
throughout the United States.

Carol Wilson
Insight Meditation Society
Pleasant Street
Barre, MA 01005
(508) 355-4378

Carol Wilson has been practicing and studying, largely in the Theravada
tradition, since 1971. She has trained with teachers from India, Burma,
Thailand, and Nepal, and she spent a year as a Buddhist nun in Thailand.
She has been teaching retreats in Vipassana intensive awareness practice
since 1986. Carol has been closely associated with the Insight Meditation
Society for many years. Currently she is a senior teacher at IMS. She also
serves on the board of directors of the Barre Center for Buddhist Studies.
She is committed to making Vipassana meditation practice accessible to
our Western culture as a vehicle for awakening.

SOUTHERN UNITED STATES

Sama Cowan
P.O. Box 3593
Fayetteville, AR 72702
(501) 443-0546

Sama Cowan was a Theravada Buddhist nun and now teaches Dharma. At her developing center she offers classes in Vipassana meditation, Buddhism, and the Pali language. Her emphasis is on the practice of Metta or lovingkindness, and she offers Sunday morning sessions on Metta meditation.

Anne Klein
Dawn Mountain
4615 Post Oak Pl., Suite 204
Houston, TX 77027-9730
(713) 222-2331

Anne Klein, Ph.D., has studied and practiced Buddhist teachings in the U.S. and Asia since 1970. Her primary teaching authorization is from the Nyingma Dzogchen Lama Khetsun Sangpo Rinboche of Kathmandu. She has studied with renowned Geluk and Dzogchen masters in Asia and the U.S. and continues to translate texts and oral commentary. She teaches at Dawn Mountain and leads semiannual weekend retreats in Chapel Hill, Texas. Her emphasis is on engaging in Tibetan practices with a sensitivity to the different strengths of women and men, and to the cultural differences between traditional Tibetan and modern practitioners. Professor and chair of the department of religious studies, Rice University, Anne's most recent book is *Meeting the Great Bliss Queen: Buddhists, Feminists, and the Art of the Self.* She is founding codirector of Dawn Mountain, a Tibetan temple, community center, and research institute.

Pat Phelan
Chapel Hill Zen Group
5322 Highway 86
Chapel Hill, NC 27514
(919) 967-0861

Pat Phelan was trained and did Zen practice for twenty years at the San Francisco Zen Center and Tassajara Zen Monastery. She was practice leader of the San Francisco Zen Center and director, before relocating to Chapel Hill. She leads the Chapel Hill Zen Group, offering all-day sittings and five-day retreats. Married and the mother of a thirteen-year-old, Pat strives in her teaching to encourage self-acceptance as a foundation for meditation practice.

Teijō
Zen Center of Asheville
P.O. Box 17274
Asheville, NC 28816-7274
(704) 253-2314

Teijō Munnich, head teacher at the Zen Center of Asheville (Magnanimous Mind Temple), dreams of starting a Women's Dharma Monastery for the cultivation of women's spirituality through Zen meditation. Teijō is an ordained student of the late Dainin Katagiri Roshi of the Minnesota Zen Meditation Center and has received additional training at Tassajara Zen Mountain Center in California and Hosshinji Sodo in Japan. She follows a traditional style of Soto Zen practice, with a personal emphasis on body/mind awareness.

MIDWEST

Diane Martin
Udumbara Sangha
501 Sherman Avenue
Evanston, IL 60202
(847) 475-3264
Fax (847) 475-8937

Diane Martin, a Soto Zen priest, has studied with teachers such as Suzuki Roshi and Katagiri Roshi. Her ordination priest is Yvonne Rand, with whom she also studied Tibetan Buddhism. Her Udumbara Sangha has branches in Lafayette and Breaux Bridge, Lousiana; Cleveland, Ohio; Mequon and Milwaukee, Wisconsin; and Cupertino, California. She travels from group to group leading sesshins, sutra studies, and training programs. Committed to engaged Buddhism, Udumbara offers a chaplaincy track for hospital, prison, and counseling work and has a unique group, the Kwan Yin Brigade, ready for any emergency. Diane is also a Jungian analyst.

Jōen Snyder O'Neal
Center for Mindful Living
3206 Holmes Avenue
Minneapolis, MN 55408
(612) 825-7658

Jōen Snyder O'Neal was trained and received Dharma transmission from Dainin Katagiri Roshi at the Minnesota Zen Center. She also has done training in the Theravadin and Vipassana traditions and has been greatly influenced by her practice at Plum Village with Thich Nhat Hanh. Jōen and her husband, Michael O'Neal, are codirectors of the Center for Mindful Living. They offer courses on Buddhism with an emphasis on mindful integration of the practice and teachings into daily life activities.

Mary Orr
3223 Redwood Drive
Aptos, CA 95003
(408) 688-3958

While her residence is in California, Mary Orr teaches principally in the Midwest and the South. Building upon her background in Western spiritual practice and Jungian psychology, she trained in the Theravada Buddhist tradition with strong Mahayana practice. She has been teaching for five or six years in Montana, North Dakota, Arkansas, Mississippi, the Kansas City area, and Iowa. She welcomes calls from interested women.

Karen Sunna
Minnesota Zen Center
3393 E. Calhoun Parkway
Minneapolis, MN 55408
(612) 822-5313

Karen Sunna has been studying and teaching for more than twenty years in the Zen lineage at the Minnesota Zen Center, where she received Dharma transmission from the late Katagiri Roshi. Now, as head of the Minnesota Zen Center, Karen is involved in creating new, more inclusive retreats and programs there.

SOUTHWEST

Tsultrim Allione
Tara Mandala Retreat Center
P.O. Box 3040
Pagosa Springs, CO 81147
(970) 264-6177
Fax (970) 264-6169

Tsultrim Allione became a Tibetan Buddhist nun at age nineteen, later disrobed, married, and raised a family. She has continued to practice under the guidance of her Tibetan Lama teachers for the past thirty years.

Recently she has established the Tara Mandala Retreat Center in the beautiful San Juan Mountains of Colorado near the Four Corners area. She offers retreats based on Dakini teachings and female-originated practices, as well as general retreats on traditional Tibetan Buddhist teachings and practices. She wrote *Women of Wisdom.*

Judith Simmer-Brown
The Naropa Institute
2130 Arapahoe Avenue
Boulder, CO 80302
(303) 546-3502

Coming from a past of feminist organizing, Judith Simmer-Brown began studying and practicing Tibetan Buddhism with Trungpa Rinpoche in 1974. She organized the first Women and Buddhism conference in 1981 at Naropa Institute in Boulder, where she has been teaching for nearly twenty years. She is chair of the institute's Religious Studies Program, and teaches Indo-Tibetan Buddhism and Meditation. In her teaching, she is very interested in integrating Buddhist practice with study. She is completing a book on feminine principle in Tibetan Buddhism.

NORTHWEST

Dr. Jan Chozen Bays
P.O. Box 310
Corbett, OR 97019
(503) 282-7879

Jan Chozen Bays trained at the Zen Center of Los Angeles and is a Dharma heir of Maezumi Roshi. She has lived in Oregon for fourteen years, where she works as a pediatrician in the area of child abuse. She is the mother of five children herself. She heads the Zen Center of Oregon and Larch Mountain Zen Center, which offer sesshins and meditation weekends. Jan conducts ceremonies for remembrance of the dead. She offers workshops and seminars for women who have been abused by Buddhist teachers and leaders. In her teaching she emphasizes two dimensions of human development: living an ethical life and cultivating insight.

Gyokuko Carlson
Dharma Rain Zen Center
2539 SE Madison Street
Portland, OR 97214
(503) 239-4846

Gyokuko Carlson has practiced and studied Zen for more than twenty years, and received Dharma transmission from Roshi Jiyu Kennett. With her husband she runs the Dharma Rain Zen Center, which offers a regular schedule of sesshins and a Dharma school for children and parents. Students work with her in a lay discipleship program. Her emphasis is integrating the practice into daily life.

Jacqueline Mandell
P.O. Box 2085
Portland, OR 97208-2085
(503) 790-1064

Jacqueline Mandell has trained in the Theravada, Mahayana, and Vajrayana traditions. For the last nine years her primary practices have come from the Tibetan Vajrayana path. She is the mother of twins. She teaches Mindfulness Awareness Meditation in teacher training sessions for people who want to teach in a Buddhist or secular setting, or who want to promote mindfulness at their job sites or in their communities.

Lama Inge Sandvoss
Padma Ling
West 1014 Seventh Avenue
Spokane, WA 99204
(509) 747-1559

Lama Inge, of German descent, is one of the first Tibetan Buddhist women lamas ordained in the United States, in the lineage of Chagdud Tulku Rinpoche. An experienced teacher, she runs the Padma Ling meditation center in Washington with her husband, Lama Yontan.

California

Joko Beck
Zen Center of San Diego
(619) 273-3444

Joko Beck studied for many years at the Los Angeles Zen Center and was given Dharma transmission there. A mother and a musician, she heads the Ordinary Mind Zen School, of which the Zen Center of San Diego is one arm. She maintains that the school is not affiliated with any religion. Her teaching focuses strongly on the living of daily existence in a Dharmic way. She is the author of *Everyday Zen: Love and Work* and *Nothing Special: Living Zen.*

Sylvia Boorstein
c/o Spirit Rock Meditation Center
P.O. Box 909
Woodacre, CA 94973
(415) 488-0164

Sylvia Boorstein is a therapist/Vipassana meditation teacher, mother, and grandmother who leads retreats and classes at Spirit Rock. She is the author of *It's Easier Than You Think*, and *Don't Just Do Something, Sit There*.

Darlene Cohen, M.A., LMT
255 Laguna Street
San Francisco, CA 94102
(415) 552-5695

Darlene Cohen, who studied Zen at San Francisco Zen Center and Green Gulch Farm, suffers from rheumatoid arthritis, a painful and crippling immune system disease. She has trained extensively in self-healing techniques and massage and movement therapy, which she combines with meditation and mindfulness exercises in her teaching. She sees private clients and gives arthritis workshops, lectures, and pain seminars emphasizing mindfulness at medical facilities and meditation centers throughout the San Francisco Bay area as well as in Spokane, Washington, and Evanston, Illinois. Her book is *Arthritis: Stop Suffering, Start Moving/Everyday Exercises for Body and Mind*.

Linda Ruth Cutts
Green Gulch Farm
1601 Shoreline Highway

Sausalito, CA 94965

(415) 383-3134

Linda Ruth Cutts is head of practice at Green Gulch Farm in Muir Beach. She has been practicing Zen since 1971, with many years of training at the San Francisco Zen Center, Green Gulch, and Tassajara Zen Monastery. She lives with her husband and their two children at Green Gulch Farm, where she leads meditation sessions, counsels individuals, and lectures about Dharma practice. Each year she co-teaches a One-day Women's Sitting and a Women's Zen Weekend workshop.

Ruth Denison

Dhamma Dena

Desert Vipassana Center

HC-1, Box 250

Joshua Tree, CA 92252

(619) 362-4815

Ruth Denison, pioneer teacher of Vipassana meditation, has been teaching for the past twenty years in North American and Europe. She is founder and resident teacher of Dhamma Dena Desert Vipassana Center, where she offers both scheduled and self-courses throughout the year, and of the Zentrum fur Buddhismus in Nickenich, Germany. She also teaches at Spirit Rock in California, Insight Meditation Society in Massachusetts, and Breitenbush Center in Oregon.

Anna Douglas

c/o Spirit Rock Meditation Center

P.O. Box 909

Woodacre, CA 94973

(415) 488-0164

Anna Douglas leads Vipassana retreats, daylongs, and classes through Spirit Rock and Insight Meditation Society in Massachusetts. She leads an annual spring women's retreat with Christina Feldman in California and also teaches nationwide. She is in the process of putting together a book of writings by women doing Dharma practice. In some of her classes she combines painting with meditation.

Palden Drolma (Caroline Alioto)
Sukhasiddhi Foundation
20 Sunnyside, Box 214
Mill Valley, CA 94941
(415)721-2952
e-mail: sukasiddhi@aol.com

Palden Drolma studied for many years in various religious traditions including Christian, Sufi, Hindu, and Native American. She has been studying and practicing Tibetan (Vajrayana) Buddhism for twenty years and is a lama in the Kagyu lineage. She works as a psychotherapist with a specialty in the interface of psychological, physical, and spiritual issues. At Sukhasiddhi Foundation, Palden teaches traditional practices within a perspective of mind, body, and spirit integration. Her teaching style incorporates a non-hierarchical feminine perspective that honors and facilitates the inner wisdom of each seeker.

Blanche Hartman
San Francisco Zen Center
300 Page Street
San Francisco, CA 94102
(415) 863-3136

Abbess of the San Francisco Zen Center, Blanche Hartman is the first woman ever to hold this post. She has practiced the Dharma for twenty-seven years and has lived at the Zen Center for twenty-four. She received Dharma transmission from Mel Weitsman. Mother of four children and grandmother of five, she leads practice periods at the San Francisco Zen Center and Tassajara Zen Monastery. In addition to her usual duties she also teaches the sewing of the traditional robes known as kesa and rakusu, an important Zen practice. She has been influenced by a number of Japanese female teachers. She is most interested in the practice of lovingkindness and compassion, taught in a traditional setting and style.

Leslie James
Tassajara Zen Mountain Center
39171 Tassajara Road
Carmel Valley, CA 93924
(415) 863-3136

Leslie James has practiced and studied Zen for many years at the San Francisco Zen Center, where she was president for six years. She is a wife and mother as well as a Zen student. Now she is director and a practice leader at Tassajara, a Zen monastery.

Wendy Johnson
Green Gulch Farm
1601 Shoreline Highway
Sausalito, CA 94965
(415) 383-3134

Longtime Zen practitioner and ordained disciple of Thich Nhat Hanh, Wendy Johnson combines ecology with Buddhism in action and teaches gardening as engaged mindfulness practice.

Roshi Jiyu Kennett

Shasta Abbey

P.O. Box 199

Mt. Shasta, CA 96067-0199

(916) 926-4208

Fax (916) 926-0428

Roshi Jiyu Kennett is the founder of Shasta Abbey, a Buddhist monastery and seminary in the Serene Reflection Meditation tradition (Chinese: Ts'ao-Tung Ch'an; Japanese: Soto Zen). Retreats are offered for laypeople at the Abbey. Roshi Jiyu Kennett is a groundbreaking teacher of the older generation. She is a musician, and at her abbey Zen texts are sung in Western plainchant, with organ accompaniment. Her books include *Zen Is Eternal Life, How to Grow a Lotus Blossom, and The Wild White Goose*, Vols. I and II.

Yvonne Rand

Goat-in-the-Road

1821 Shoreline Highway

Muir Beach, CA 94965

(415) 388-5572

Fax (415) 388-9615

Yvonne Rand is a meditation teacher and a lay householder priest in the Soto Zen tradition. She incorporates practices and teachings from the Vipassana and Tibetan Buddhist traditions also. She has been studying and practicing meditation for more than thirty years. She now leads retreats in her own meditation center, Goat-in-the-Road, as well as a meditation, lecture, and discussion group in Berkeley for women. For a "Calendar of Events with Yvonne Rand," call or write her center.

Diane Rizzetto
Bay Zen Center
5600A Snake Road
Oakland, CA 94611
(510) 482-2533

Diane Rizzetto began Zen practice at the Berkeley Zen Center with Sojun Mel Weitsman. Continuing her training for many years with Charlotte Joko Beck of the San Diego Zen Center, she received Dharma transmission from Joko and assumed teaching leadership of the Bay Zen Center. She is the mother of three children and grandmother of four. The Bay Zen Center is open to people of all traditions and offers a full schedule of sesshins, daily zazen, and interviews with the teacher. The practice extends into daily activities—family, relationships, the workplace, community—and the sangha seeks to support participants in realizing that true liberation rests in bringing attention to the present in any event and in any moment of their lives.

Maylie Scott
Berkeley Zen Center
1931 Russell Street
Berkeley, CA 94703
(510) 845-2403

Maylie Scott, Zen priest, teaches at the Berkeley Zen Center and heads the Arcata Zen Group. She is strongly affiliated with the Buddhist Peace Fellowship, doing antinuclear work and outreach into troubled areas of the community. Her major focus is "engaged Buddhism," which seeks to integrate meditation practice with social service.

Rina Sircar
Taungpulu Kaba-Aye Meditation Center
3494 Twenty-First Street
San Francisco, CA 94110
(415) 282-3124

Born and raised in Burma, Rina Sircar was invited to San Francisco in 1973 to teach Buddhist studies by the late Haridas Chaudhuri, founder of the California Institute of Integral (formerly Asian) Studies. Rina is a core faculty member of this accredited graduate school and holds the World Peace Buddhist Studies Chair in the Philosophy and Religion Department. In 1978 she cofounded the Taungpulu Kaba-Aye Monastery in Boulder Creek, California, with her teacher the Very Venerable Taungpulu Kaba-Aye Sayadaw Phaya. Her ministry as a Ten Precept Holder includes teaching Buddhism and vipassana meditation, healing, visiting the sick and dying, and performing weddings, funerals, and naming ceremonies.

Dr. Thynn Thynn
352 Pleasant Hill Avenue N.
Sebastopol, CA 95472
(707) 829-9857

Dr. Thynn Thynn comes from Burma where she has studied and practiced extensively with monk-teachers. She is a medical doctor and mother who teaches how to apply meditation within the full responsibilities of job and family. She teaches independently in California. Her book is *Living Meditation, Living Insight.*

Julie Wester
c/o Spirit Rock Meditation Center
P.O. Box 909
Woodacre, CA 94973
(415) 488-0164

A practitioner of vipassana since 1973, Julie Wester has been leading retreats since 1985. She is a member of the Teachers Council of Spirit Rock Center where she leads retreats for women and is actively involved in the development of the family program. She is the mother of a young daughter. Her teaching, incorporating guided movement and sensory exploration within the silent retreat format, reflects her training with Ruth Denison.

HAWAII

Kamala Masters
P.O. Box 2523
Wailuku, HI 96793

Kamala is an Asian-American mother of four children. Active in her community, she leads a local sitting group weekly and periodically offers mindfulness-based stress reduction at the local medical clinic on Maui. Her Dharma practice began with the Indian Theravada teacher Munindra more than twenty years ago, and in recent years she has continued to receive instruction in intensive retreats from Sayadaw U Pandita with whom she has practiced both insight (vipassana) and lovingkindness (metta) meditations. She now conducts retreats to share the Dharma in Minneapolis, Vancouver, B.C., Australia, New Zealand, and Barre, Massachusetts.

Karma Lekshe Tsomo
400 Hobron Lane #2615
Honolulu, HI 96815

Karma Lekshe Tsomo is an American nun practicing primarily in the Tibetan tradition. She lectures widely and teaches philosophy for the Antioch Buddhist Studies Program in Bodhgaya. She has helped develop six monastic study centers for Tibetan and Himalayan nuns in India. Her books include *Sakyadhita: Daughters of the Buddha, Buddhism Through American Women's Eyes, Sisters in Solitude,* and *The Feminization of Buddhism.* She was one of the founders of Sakyadhita: International Association of Buddhist Women.

Michelle McDonald-Smith
Vipassana Hawaii Foundation
380 Portlock Rd.
Honolulu, HI 96825

Michele McDonald-Smith has practiced vipassana meditation since 1975 and has been teaching at the insight Meditation Society in Massachusetts and worldwide since 1982. She is also a guiding teacher for Vipassana Hawaii and the Blue Mountain Vipassana Center in Australia. She has a deep interest in preserving the ancient teachings and in finding ways of expression that make them more accessible and authentic in our time. To this end her current teaching focuses on the interweaving of nature, spirituality, and poetry.

INTERNATIONAL

Pema Chodron
Gampo Abbey
Pleasant Bay
Nova Scotia BOE 2PO
Canada
(902) 224-2752
Fax (902) 224-1521
e-mail: Gampo@Shambhala.org

Pema Chodron, a student of Trungpa Rinpoche, is the director of Gampo Abbey, a monastery and retreat center in the Tibetan Buddhist tradition. She divides her time between teaching and doing personal retreats at the abbey and traveling to teach in North America and Europe. She has been a fully ordained nun since 1981 and has been wearing the robes since 1974. Her relating to people through Dharma counseling is important to her, as she attempts to make the teachings of the Buddha relevant to the suffering that people encounter. She is the author of *The Wisdom of No Escape*, *Start Where You Are*, and *When Things Fall Apart*.

Tsering Everest
Chagdud Gonpa Odsal Ling
Rua Porto Uniao, 39
Brooklin CEP 04568-020
Sao Paulo, SP
Brazil
011 55 11 535-0494

or, in the United States at
Rigdzin Ling
P.O. Box 279
Junction City, CA 96048-0279

Tsering Everest is an American woman who has been for many years the translator for the Tibetan Lama, Chagdud Tulku Rinpoche. Married and a mother, she managed to do a three-year retreat in her own home while maintaining her relationship with her family. She teaches and leads retreats. Recently Chagdud Tulku ordained her as a lama. She now teaches in Brazil but returns periodically to California.

Christina Feldman
Gaia House
Woodland Road
Denbury, Newton Abbot
Devon PQ126DY
England

Christina Feldman, an Englishwoman, studied in the Theravada and Mahayana traditions in India and has trained in Tibetan Buddhism. She teaches in the Vipassana tradition in the United States at Spirit Rock in California, with Anna Douglas, and at the Insight Meditation Society in Barre, Massachusetts. She is the author of *Woman Awake*, *The Quest of the Warrior Woman*, and *Stories of the Spirit, Stories of the Heart* with Jack Kornfield. Christina is a wife and mother as well as a Dharma teacher.

Jetsun Kushok Chime Luding
Sakya Tsechen Thubten Ling Center
7340 Frobisher Drive

Richmond, B.C. V7C 4N5

Canada

(604) 275-1915

Fax (604) 275-1989

e-mail: sakya@unixg.ubc.ca

Tibetan by birth, Jetsun-ma is a fully empowered Sakya lineage holder, trained from the age of six in the Tibetan Buddhist tradition. She is one of three women in the history of Tibet to transmit the complete cycle of Sakya teachings. Mother of five, with a full-time job, Jetsun-ma is able to guide meditators in bringing practice into their daily lives. She functions as an example and aide to women practitioners, giving the teachings in a traditional way.

A meditation center has been set up for her in the San Francisco Bay Area, where she visits frequently. Called Sakya Decheng Ling Meditation Center, it can be contacted at (510) 465-7849.

Ayya Khema

Buddha Haus

Uttenbuehl 5

87466

Oy-Mittelberg

Germany

011-49-8376-502

Fax 011-49-8376-592

Ayya Khema, a fully ordained Theravada nun, is founder of Parappu-duwa Nuns Island in Sri Lanka; Wat Buddha Dhamma in Australia; Buddha Haus and Metta Vihara forest monastery, both in Southern Germany. German-born, now an American citizen, she ran a farm and raised a family in Australia before becoming a Buddhist nun. She leads meditation retreats throughout Europe, Australia, and the United States. Her books include *Being Nobody, Going Nowhere* and *When the Iron Eagle Flies*, as well as more than a dozen books in German, which are available in nine languages, including Chinese.

Lisa Leghorn
Chagdud Gompa Brasil
CX Postal 121
95660-000 Tres Coroas, RS
Brazil
011 55 51 546 1563

Lisa Leghorn comes from a background of feminist activism in the battered women's movement and feels a sense of responsibility to the feminist community to offer the Tibetan Buddhist teachings to women as a way to transform consciousness. She received her training with Chagdud Tulku Rinpoche and teaches within the Vajrayana tradition. She travels to the twenty-one centers established by Chagdud in order to lead retreats. Her California contact is Rigdzin Ling (916) 623-2714.

Gesshin Prabhasa Dharma Roshi
International Zen Institute of America
P.O. Box 491218
Los Angeles, CA 90049
(310) 472-5707
or
Z.I.D.
c/o Dharma Padma Nicolai
Lattenkamp 70

22299 Hamburg
Germany
011 49 40 514-2316

Venerable Gesshin Prabhasa Dharma Roshi is an authorized Zen master, poet, and painter. She has been teaching Zen for more than twenty years in North America and Europe. She founded the International Zen Institute of America and Europe, which became a regional center of the World Fellowship of Buddhists and has participated in the world ecumenical movement, dialoguing with other religious traditions. She teaches Zen retreats in California, Florida, Colorado; in Spain, Holland, and Germany. She works to encourage understanding between religious traditions and to bring the practice into the lives of laypeople.

Jane Tromge
Chagdud Gonpa Brasil
CX. Postal 121
95660-000 Tres Coroas, RS
011 55 51 546-1563

Wife of Chagdud Tulku Rinpoche, Jane Tromge teaches and writes about Tibetan Buddhism.

Publications with Retreat Schedules, and Buddhist Centers Offering Retreats by Women

De Tiltenberg
Zilkerduinweg 375
2114 AM Vogelenzang
Nederland

Offers Zen retreats and programs

Inquiring Mind: A Semi-Annual Journal of the Vipassana Community.
P.O. Box 9999
North Berkeley Station
Berkeley, CA 94709

Interracial Buddhist Council
Contact: Lewis Aframi
c/o the Buddhist Peace Fellowship
P.O. Box 4650
Berkeley, CA 94704

Mid America Dharma Group
13741 Pembroke Circle
Leawood, KS 66224

Northwest Dharma Association
4020 Leary Way N.W. #360
Seattle, WA 98107

Parallax Press
c/o Community of Mindful Living
P.O. Box 7355
Berkeley, CA 94707

Most books by Thich Nhat Hanh

Sakyadhita: International Association of Buddhist Women
400 Hobron Lane #2615
Honolulu, HI 96815
Membership and dues: Sierra Crawford
P.O. Box 8585, Emeryville, CA 94662-8585. (510) 655-4781

Shambhala Sun
1585 Barrington Street, Suite 300
Halifax, Nova Scotia
Canada B3J 1Z8
U.S. Office: 1345 Spruce Street, Boulder, CO 80301-4886

Shasta Abbey Press
P.O. Box 199, Dept. FC
Mt. Shasta, CA 96067-0199

Snow Lion Newsletter and Catalog
P.O. Box 6483
Ithaca, NY 143851

Southern Dharma Retreat Center
Route 1, Box 34H
Hot Springs, NC 28743
(704) 622-7112

Spirit Rock Meditation Center Newsletter
c/o Spirit Rock Meditation Center
P.O. Box 909
Woodacre, CA 94973

Tara Mandala Newsletter
P.O. Box 3040
Pagosa Springs, CO 81147

tricycle: the Buddhist Review
92 Vandam Street
New York, NY 10013

Turning Wheel: Journal of the Buddhist Peace Fellowship
P.O. Box 4650
Berkeley, CA 94704

Chapters and affiliates throughout the United States and some other countries. Write to the above address for listing.

Books and Articles for Further Reading

I have cited these books and articles in the text and offer them here for your further information.

CHAPTER I

May, Herbert G., and Bruce M. Metzger, eds. *The New Oxford Annotated Bible.* Revised standard version. New York: Oxford University Press, 1977.

CHAPTER II

Yu, Chun-fang. "Feminine Images of Kuan-Yin in Post-Tang China." *Journal of Chinese Religions* 18 (fall 1990).

Nhat Hanh, Thich. *A Guide to Walking Meditation.* Translated by Jenny Hoang and Nguyen Anh Huong. Nyack, N.Y.: Fellowship Publications, 1985.

CHAPTER III

Horner, I. B. *Women Under Primitive Buddhism.* Delhi: Motilal Banarsidass, 1930, 1975.

Rhys Davids, Mrs. M.A., *Psalms of the Early Buddhists. I.-Psalms of the Sisters.* Henry Frowde for the Pali Text Society. England: Oxford University Press Warehouse, 1909.

Paul, Diana Y. *Women in Buddhism: Images of the Feminine in Mahayana Tradition.* Berkeley: Asian Humanities Press, 1979.

Shaw, Miranda. *Passionate Enlightenment: Women in Tantric Buddhism.* Princeton, N.J.: Princeton University Press, 1994.

CHAPTER IV

Kennett, Roshi Jiyu. *Zen Is Eternal Life.* Emeryville, Calif.: Dharma Publishing, 1976.

Hixon, Lex. *Coming Home: The Experience of Enlightenment in Sacred Traditions.* New York: J. P. Tarcher, 1989.

Index

prejudice against women, 91–
94
sadhanas, 89
variety, 3

Cabinet, wooden (gohonzon),
30–31
Caring for others, 124, 126
Catholic faith. *See* Christianity
Celestial bodhisattvas, 88, 95–96
Change. *See* Impermanence
Chanting, 29, 31. *See also* Bud-
dhist songs
to Tara, 65
Charity. *See* Dana (generosity)
Chodron, Pema, 53
Christianity, 52
beliefs about suffering, 106
Bible vs. Buddhist texts, 9–10
contrasts with Buddhism, 8,
16
goddess vestiges, 55
Clarity. *See* Enlightenment
Clinging, 124. *See also* Desire;
Impermanence
Coming Home (Lex Hixon), 129
Community. *See* Sangha
Compassion, 12, 13–14, 26–28,
126–30
meditation for, 100–103

Concentration, increasing, 103.
See also Right Concen-
tration
Conduct, code for Buddhist Cen-
ters, 52
Conduct, right. *See* Morality
Conferences on Women and Bud-
dhism, 50–51
Consciousness, 15
Contents of Mind, 131
Courtesans, enlightenment, 81
Craving, 108. *See also* Desire

Daily life, 11, 15, 26, 32–35. *See also*
Domesticity; Living in the
moment; Samsara
Dakinis, 61–62
Dana (generosity), 15, 84–85
Dancing, 118
Daughters of the Buddha
(Sakyadhita), 98
Deliverance. *See* Liberation
Denison, Ruth, 2, 3, 13, 44–45, 48–
49, 105, 116, 131
Desire, 17–23, 33–34, 68, 107–8
monks' for women, 92
Detachment, 82, 123–24
Dhammadinna, 75
Dharma, 12
as teacher, 117